PAINTING

by Don Nardo

LUCENT BOOKS
A part of Gale, Cengage Learning

Detroit • New York • San Francisco • New Haven, Conn • Waterville, Maine • London

LIBRARY OF CONGRESS CATALOGING-IN-PUBLICATION DATA

Nardo, Don, 1947-
  Painting / by Don Nardo.
     p. cm. -- (Eye on art)
  Includes bibliographical references and index.
  ISBN 978-1-4205-0549-8 (hardcover)
  1. Painting--History. I. Title.
  ND50.N37 2012
  759--dc23

                                                              2011039198

Lucent Books
27500 Drake Rd
Farmington Hills MI 48331

ISBN-13: 978-1-4205-0549-8
ISBN-10: 1-4205-0549-1

Printed in the United States of America
2 3 4 5 6 7 15 14 13 12

CONTENTS

Foreword

"Art has no other purpose than to brush aside . . . everything that veils reality from us in order to bring us face to face with reality itself."

—French philosopher Henri-Louis Bergson

Some thirty-one thousand years ago, early humans painted strikingly sophisticated images of horses, bison, rhinoceroses, bears, and other animals on the walls of a cave in southern France. The meaning of these elaborate pictures is unknown, although some experts speculate that they held ceremonial significance. Regardless of their intended purpose, the Chauvet-Pont-d'Arc cave paintings represent some of the first known expressions of the artistic impulse.

From the Paleolithic era to the present day, human beings have continued to create works of visual art. Artists have developed painting, drawing, sculpture, engraving, and many other techniques to produce visual representations of landscapes, the human form, religious and historical events, and countless other subjects. The artistic impulse also finds expression in glass, jewelry, and new forms inspired by new technology. Indeed, judging by humanity's prolific artistic output throughout history, one must conclude that the compulsion to produce art is an inherent aspect of being human, and the results are among humanity's greatest cultural achievements: masterpieces such as the architectural marvels of ancient Greece, Michelangelo's perfectly rendered statue *David*, Vincent van Gogh's visionary painting *Starry Night*, and endless other treasures.

The creative impulse serves many purposes for society. At its most basic level, art is a form of entertainment or the means for a satisfying or pleasant aesthetic experience. But art's true power lies not in its potential to entertain and delight but in its ability to enlighten, to reveal the truth, and by doing so to uplift the human spirit and transform the human race.

One of the primary functions of art has been to serve religion. For most of Western history, for example, artists were paid by the church to produce works with religious themes and subjects. Art was thus a tool to help human beings transcend mundane, secular reality and achieve spiritual enlightenment. One of the best-known, and largest-scale, examples of Christian religious art is the Sistine Chapel in the Vatican in Rome. In 1508 Pope Julius II commissioned Italian Renaissance artist Michelangelo to paint the chapel's vaulted ceiling, an area of 640 square yards (535 sq. m). Michelangelo spent four years on scaffolding, his neck craned, creating a panoramic fresco of some three hundred human figures. His paintings depict Old Testament prophets and heroes, sibyls of Greek mythology, and nine scenes from the Book of Genesis, including the Creation of Adam, the Fall of Adam and Eve from the Garden of Eden, and the Flood. The ceiling of the Sistine Chapel is considered one of the greatest works of Western art and has inspired the awe of countless Christian pilgrims and other religious seekers. As eighteenth-century German poet and author Johann Wolfgang von Goethe wrote, "Until you have seen this Sistine Chapel, you can have no adequate conception of what man is capable of."

In addition to inspiring religious fervor, art can serve as a force for social change. Artists are among the visionaries of any culture. As such, they often perceive injustice and wrongdoing and confront others by reflecting what they see in their work. One classic example of art as social commentary was created in May 1937, during the brutal Spanish civil war. On May 1 Spanish artist Pablo Picasso learned of the recent attack on the small Basque village of Guernica by German airplanes allied with fascist forces led by Francisco Franco. The German pilots had used the village for target practice, a three-hour bombing that killed sixteen hundred civilians. Picasso, living in Paris, channeled his outrage over the massacre into his painting *Guernica,* a black, white, and gray mural that depicts dismembered animals and fractured human figures whose faces are contorted in agonized expressions. Initially, critics and the public condemned the painting as an incoherent hodgepodge, but the work soon came to be seen as a powerful antiwar statement and remains an iconic symbol of the violence and terror that dominated world events during the remainder of the twentieth century.

The impulse to create art—whether painting animals with crude pigments on a cave wall, sculpting a human form from marble, or commemorating human tragedy in a mural—thus serves many purposes. It offers an entertaining diversion, nourishes the imagination and the spirit, decorates and beautifies the world, and chronicles the age. But underlying all these functions is the desire to reveal that which is obscure—to illuminate, clarify, and perhaps ennoble. As Picasso himself stated, "The purpose of art is washing the dust of daily life off our souls."

The Eye on Art series is intended to assist readers in understanding the various roles of art in society. Each volume offers an in-depth exploration of a major artistic movement, medium, figure, or profession. All books in the series are beautifully illustrated with full-color photographs and diagrams. Riveting narrative, clear technical explanation, informative sidebars, fully documented quotes, a bibliography, and a thorough index all provide excellent starting points for research and discussion. With these features, the Eye on Art series is a useful introduction to the world of art—a world that can offer both insight and inspiration.

Introduction

A Mirror of Human Culture

Today, the idea is widely accepted that painters and other artists pursue their craft or art mainly because they are emotionally or psychologically driven to do so. That is, they have feelings, ideas, or some other personal outlook or vision to express. Painting pictures, it seems, is the best way they know how to pursue such individual expression and make their own individual mark in the world. Thus, people who view a painting commonly ask what the artist's vision or intent was in creating it. "What were you trying to say in that painting?" or words to that effect, is a question frequently posed to modern painters.

This way of looking at the art of painting is based on the notion that it has always been primarily a form of personal expression. Similarly, it is assumed that people have always looked at and/or bought and hung paintings because they were touched by or "got" whatever the artist was trying to say in the work. Or else they bought the painting, or went to see it in a museum, simply because they felt it was visually beautiful or striking.

A third market—or outlet or reason for creation—for paintings is financial in nature. It involves some people's buying these artworks because they were created by well-known artists. In that case, owning a painting is a matter of investing in an object worth a lot of money, mostly because art critics and appraisers say that is the case. In addition, besides the monetary value, owning a work by a famous artist can significantly increase one's prestige or social stature.

The reality of the history of painting markets is very different, however. Most of these factors, including art critics, world famous painters, paintings worth a lot of money, and painting mainly as a form of personal expression, did not exist

Until the nineteenth century, wealthy patrons, nobility, and the clergy commissioned most major artworks and played an active role in the development of the work.

before early modern times. As art critic and historian Robert Cumming points out,

> Before the 19th century and the development of the modern [art] dealers' network, most major works of art were commissioned by a patron who would often specify exacting conditions or play an active role in shaping the subject matter and appearance of a work. The majority of early patrons [in late medieval and early modern Europe] were the Catholic Church and the royal courts of Europe. Only after the Romantic movement of the early 19th century does the role of the artist as a solitary individual creating a private vision begin to emerge.[1]

Functional Rather than Emotional

A brief look at the historical evolution of painting markets illustrates how singular and special painters of today and the potential outlets for their works are compared with those in past ages. Indeed, for untold centuries, paintings were viewed almost entirely as functional objects. "Art as we know it now," one expert writes, "was not a consideration. Simple competence was sufficient."[2] The reason was that those who hired painters had specific and mainly practical reasons for doing so. Their emotions, and certainly the painters' emotions and feelings, had nothing to do with it.

An early example consists of the wall paintings produced in ancient Crete and Egypt in the second millennium B.C. and by the Mayans in Central America in the first millennium A.D. Most had mainly religious themes, including depictions of gods and worship and scenes from mythology. The painters created these works at the behest of local religious leaders, who had the good of the community in mind. The intention was to seek the favor of a god or gods so that such deities would look kindly on that community, not to create something pretty to look at or to cater to the artists' feelings or needs.

One exception to this early functional kind of painting market consisted of a few Cretan paintings. They were done on the walls of the homes of some of the community's well-to-do and appear to have been at least partly meant as decoration. On a considerably larger scale, such decorative needs became another practical market for painters in ancient Greece and Rome. Some Greek painters were primarily potters who used paint to decorate their cups, bowls, and vases with scenes from mythology and everyday life. Once again, there was no intent or expectation to create "great art" (although later ages did come to see much

Some of the earliest known wall paintings have been found in Crete. They usually contain religious or mythical themes.

of that pottery as just that). The potter-painters, along with the Greek and Roman painters who created murals, were hired to do a job—to create functional decorations for homes or public buildings.

In most cases, only well-to-do folk could afford to hire painters to do murals. In fact, throughout most of history the majority of those who commissioned paintings were members of the upper classes. In early China, for instance, the principal form of painting—done in ink on sheets of silk—was fashioned almost exclusively for the emperor and his rich nobles. European nobility, from the Roman emperors to the kings, dukes, and of lords of medieval times, formed a similarly limited and wealthy market for paintings.

Medieval Europe also possessed a second major market that called on the services of people with painting talent. Namely, Christian bishops and priests wanted to decorate the interiors of their churches but not simply to beautify them. The most important reason was to provide illiterate worshippers with a way of learning about Bible stories. Bibles illustrated with miniature paintings, called "illuminations," were another such medieval market for painters' works. As one might expect, those artists had little or no say in choosing their subjects. The paintings "had to be acceptable to the church fathers," says cultural observer John Graham.

> Furthermore, the church had rules of what constituted an acceptable religious painting, and these became restrictions to free expression and any progress in painting. [Also] the humans in paintings showed no emotion. Thus, even though the church preserved the techniques of painting for five hundred years, it stifled creativity for the same period.[3]

Paintings Become Democratic

Several new painting markets emerged following the Reformation, the great separation of Protestant churches from the Roman Catholic Church in the 1500s and 1600s. Most early

Protestant leaders viewed colorful church decorations as either too gaudy or as sinful. In fact, a number of religious paintings and other works of art were destroyed by overzealous ministers and worshippers during these years.

As a result, most painters steered clear of the church. They managed to find a new market in the form of portraits and other portable (easily carried) pictures for private upper- and upper-middle-class families. These typically hung above mantlepieces, in foyers, or on the walls lining staircases in homes both in cities and the countryside. Home owners commissioned such pieces for prestige—to show off their families, horses, and other "possessions" to others—or to capture family memories. This marked the beginning of the custom of decorating the walls of homes with portable paintings of various sizes, which steadily spread to middle-class and even lower-middle-class homes.

Coming close on the heels of this development was the rise of art academies in London, Paris, Amsterdam, and other major European cities in the 1700s. Not only did young painters train in these schools, the academies also held annual exhibitions of the "best" paintings produced by artists young and old. More and more, so-called art experts—commonly called "critics"—emerged to decide which paintings and their creators were better than others. In turn, this stimulated the appearance of still another major painting market—art collectors, who sought paintings in large part as investments or prestige objects. Both collectors and critics began opening art galleries in the big cities, where the public could view the latest paintings. In this way, many individual painters gained names recognized by society and could command fees that artists in prior ages could only dream about.

Finally, in the 1800s and on into the 1900s, numerous "niche" markets opened up for painters. These included the need for illustrations for mass-market books and pamphlets; art for theater and movie posters; drawings for comic books, which eventually grew into graphic novels; art for billboard, magazine, TV, and Internet ads; and inexpensive reproductions of popular or classic paintings. These and other modern markets made large numbers of paintings affordable to millions of people of average or lower-than-average means.

In a way, then, the progression of painting markets over time made paintings, and art in general, more democratic, or more accessible to large numbers of average people. At the same time, it made it possible for individual painters to have a chance for recognition, prosperity, and self-fulfillment. Today, unlike the situation throughout most of history, a painter can pursue his or her calling to satisfy an emotional need and maybe make a living at it, too. At the same time, society has become culturally richer as it has learned to appreciate art merely for its inherent beauty and worth, while nurturing talented individuals in its midst. In the words of art historian Hans L.C. Jaffe,

> Through its increased accessibility, and because of the progress made in the techniques of reproduction [for the masses], painting in recent [times] has become a mirror of human culture in which in each generation, every individual [painter] strives for self-discovery. [The] wide-ranging history of painting . . . therefore has meaning and importance not only for the historical sciences, but even more for our present-day cultural consciousness.[4]

The Earliest Civilizations: The Dawn of Painting

What the first painted images looked like and the exact materials used to create them are lost in the mists of time. The identities of the people who produced those images are also a mystery that will likely never be solved. More certain is that those inventive individuals lived long before the first major, centralized civilizations emerged in river valleys in Mesopotamia (now Iraq), Egypt, India, and China. Eventually, these and a few other early cultures independently produced the first organized painting traditions. Each tradition consisted of certain materials and techniques that were passed on from one generation to the next. Once established, such a tradition often influenced cultures in neighboring areas, and in this way the art of painting steadily spread across large parts of the world.

Of these early painting traditions, perhaps the oldest and certainly the most diverse and well known is the one that grew up in the West, centered on Europe and its periphery (including Egypt). The Western painting tradition is also the longest unbroken one in history. In addition, it was the first one to produce a large network of art schools, galleries, critics, and collectors. For these reasons, much of painting's history revolves around European painters and their styles and works.

From Beneath the Earth

Some important clues to the enduring mystery of the beginnings of the art of painting, both in the West and elsewhere, emerged in September 1940. Late in that month Marcel Ravidat, Jacques Marsal, and two other teenage boys anxiously searched for their dog Robot, who had recently gone missing in the woods near the town of Montignac, in western France. Finally, they heard the pup's muffled barks and realized, to their surprise, that they were coming from beneath the earth. Following the sounds, they came upon a hole in the ground formed by an uprooted tree. It was clear that Robot had fallen into the dark fissure and become trapped. The boys slipped down into the hole, and Marsal later recalled the ordeal, saying, "the descent was terrifying."[5] About 50 feet (15m) down,

In the Lascaux Cave in France prehistoric artists created over two thousand images of horses, bison, and other beasts more than seventeen thousand years ago.

they found Robot in an underground cavern that soon came to be known as the Lascaux Cave.

In the process of rescuing the much-relieved canine, the boys made one of the most important historical and cultural discoveries of modern times. To their amazement, they saw a series of magnificent paintings on the cave's rock walls. Marsal later described them as a "cavalcade of animals larger than life painted on the walls and ceiling of the cave. Each animal seemed to be moving."[6] The painted animals and the feeling of movement Marsal described were more recently explained by *National Geographic* reporter Andrew Howley:

> When you first enter the cave, on the upper part of the left wall and on to the ceiling is a series of horses. . . . There are eight of them of varying levels of detail, completion, and preservation, but what is most striking is that the legs of each are in different positions in the gait of a running horse. In the complete darkness of a cave, [a] candle moved along the wall would show each of these in succession, providing a highly evocative [descriptive] sense of the motion of one animal running along the wall and receding into the distance.[7]

Scientists have determined that Lascaux's roughly two thousand images of horses, bison, and other beasts were created about seventeen thousand years ago. The prehistoric artists employed local natural materials, including charcoal and various powdered minerals mixed with animal fat or spit. The drawings were not meant merely as decoration. Rather, as art historian Roy Bolton points out, "they were serving that magical or religious part of mankind that has propelled the arts through most ages. Painting the beasts of the kill was probably their way of magically trapping them."[8]

Lascaux is not the only cave in which prehistoric rock paintings have been found. Even older images of animals rendered by early hunter-gatherers came to light in 1994 in the Chauvet Cave in southern France. Similar finds have been made in Spain and other parts of Europe, as well as farther

THE FRAGILE CAVE PAINTINGS THREATENED

The rock paintings in France's Lascaux Cave are extremely fragile. Back in 1940, when he and his three friends found the cave, Jacques Marsal recognized the importance of the paintings and worried about their safety. He pitched a tent at the cave's entrance and thereafter made it his life's work to guard the paintings, as well as show them to eager visitors from around the world. Eventually, as a spokesperson for the International Committee for Preservation of Lascaux explains, various hazards threatened the paintings, forcing French authorities to close the cave to the public.

Carbon dioxide, from the breath of thousands [of visitors], began to build in the cave. At times, carbon dioxide levels were so high that visitors passed out from the toxicity. Worse yet, condensation formed on the walls and ceilings of the cave causing moisture to run down the precious paintings. The Green Sickness, a green growth on the walls and paintings, was one of the first signs of how human presence adversely affects the cave's health. High temperatures and humidity, together with high levels of carbon dioxide, [also took a toll]. In 1963, France's Minister of Culture . . . closed the cave to the public. [After that] Lascaux remained closed to all but a small group of researchers and scientists. It is now closed to all but its caretakers.

International Committee for Preservation of Lascaux. "Finding Lascaux: Four Boys and a Dog." www.save lascaux.org/Legacy_Finding.php.

south, on the African continent. Namibia, in southwestern Africa, has rock paintings of animals and people dating back some twenty-seven thousand years. No less exciting to anthropologists and art historians alike were more than thirty thousand cave and rock paintings discovered in scattered locales in the Drakensberg Mountains in South Africa. Using dyes made from berries, plants, and animal parts, some of the region's earliest residents crafted lasting images of the creatures with which they shared their world.

On the Nile's Banks

It is uncertain whether these archaic southern African pictures, or knowledge of the methods that created them, influenced the creation of the world's earliest-known long-lasting painting tradition. It emerged further north, in Egypt, in Africa's northeastern corner. There, between 5000 and 4000 B.C. (six to seven thousand years ago), a well-ordered and eventually splendid agricultural society grew up along the banks of the mighty Nile River.

At first, the early Egyptians dwelled in small villages. But over time these became organized into two rival kingdoms, one in northern Egypt, the other in the south. Circa 3100 B.C. the two realms merged, producing the world's first-known nation-state. In the centuries that followed, the Egyptians fashioned one of the world's first empires and produced intermittent bursts of high culture. This included various forms of art, including

These tools and minerals were used to make paint in ancient Egypt. Pigments were combined with water and glue to make paint.

large-scale architecture, like the renowned giant pyramids and massive temples honoring the Egyptian gods. It also included magnificent sculptures, exemplified by the Great Sphinx and other huge stone statues of the Egyptian kings called pharaohs.

Painting was another major facet of art in ancient Egypt. At some unknown point in its history, a small number of its people with artistic talent learned to make pigments from common substances they found in nature. They used iron oxide and other minerals to produce red, brown, and yellow, for example, and copper ore and mineral salts to make blue. After assembling the pigments, they combined them with water and glue to make their paints. Their brushes were fashioned from the stems of Nile marsh reeds. A painter typically placed assorted globs of these paints on a palette made of wood or pottery, held the palette in one hand, and wielded his brush with the other. Thus, the basic tools and methods used by Egyptian painters were very much like those employed by their modern counterparts.

Following Strict Conventions

Very much *un*like today's artists, however, those in ancient Egypt did not paint whatever subjects they wanted. Nor could they experiment with different styles and methods, as modern painters can and often do. Instead, Egyptian painters strictly followed a set of traditional, accepted rules and techniques collectively called conventions.

Today, the best-known of these conventions is the one that dictated the manner in which painters portrayed the human body. Appropriately, it is often called the "Egyptian pose" or "Egyptian style." Art historian Dianne Durante describes it, saying,

> Almost without exception, the head is represented from a side view in a stark outline. Normally, in a profile image only half the eye is seen. In an Egyptian profile, however, the whole eye stares out from the side of the head at the viewer. Similarly, the body and legs are in profile, but the torso is turned fully to the front, making the figure's body appear uncomfortably twisted, despite the desire to represent a strong, powerful figure. Walking

figures have both feet flat on the ground, rather than having part of one foot lifted.[9]

The reason for this unusual way of showing the body was that the Egyptians viewed the art of painting in a highly formal, intellectual manner. They had no interest in depicting people exactly as they appeared in life. Rather, they preferred to capture a person's essence, his or her "humanness," or basic human qualities, those standard attributes that were unchanging from one generation to the next. As one art expert puts it, in Egyptian paintings "objects are presented as they are conceived [in the mind], not as they are seen." Moreover, "the desire to show all the essential characteristics of the human figure in a single image led the Egyptian artists to present it in an unnatural way."[10]

Egyptian painters strictly followed a set of traditional, accepted rules and techniques called conventions. One convention was to always paint the head and legs in profile with the torso turned to the front.

This is why those talented ancient painters depicted human figures in a standardized, formal pose that remained the same for many centuries.

Another accepted convention followed by Egyptian painters was the way they arranged figures and objects on a wall or other surface to be painted. Nearly always, they divided these subjects into horizontal bands called registers. A painted wall might have only one register or it might feature several, each arrayed above or below another. Also, the registers were arranged in a chronological sequence in order to tell a story. The events in the paintings in the lowest register on a wall were viewed as the most recent, for instance. Furthermore, within a given register the paintings situated nearest to the largest figure (almost always the pharaoh or other high-placed official) were supposed to show the most recent events. The observer assumed that the paintings placed further away from the central figure depicted older events.

Painting for the Dead

Ancient Egyptian painters were also constrained and limited by the settings in which their works appeared. With very few exceptions, officials at the royal palace, priests of a temple built to honor a certain god, or the family of a dead person hired an artist to complete a specific project. Paintings adorning the walls of palaces or temples were common projects. These depicted the pharaoh and/or members of his family, battles and other important national events, and scenes showing various gods and events from popular mythology.

The bulk of the rest of the painting jobs involved the creation of tomb paintings. The ancient Egyptians were extremely preoccupied with the concept of the afterlife and preparations for it. They believed that fashioning tomb paintings of people engaged in planting, plowing, harvesting, hunting, and fishing would ensure that those activities would continue in the afterlife. Moreover, painted images of tools, food, chariots, and other objects would supposedly come to life after the tomb was sealed. The deceased individual would therefore have access to these things in the afterlife. In this way, Durante says, "painting helped

Because they thought that, after death, their rulers would continue to live exactly as they had in this life, ancient Egyptians painted on their rulers' tomb walls what they believed they would need in the afterlife.

Egyptians document this life and 'keep alive' the world for the dead."[11] Thus, a major proportion of Egyptian art—no matter what subject was depicted—was concerned with religion and life after death.

The fact that so many Egyptian paintings were done in tombs turned out to be a stroke of luck for art lovers and historians in later ages. Almost all of the pictures painted for palaces and other structures that were exposed to the ravages of weather, the elements, and warfare and other human activities have long since disappeared. In contrast, many Egyptian tomb paintings have endured because the thick layers of rock and earth surrounding these compartments protected them.

Painting in Minoan Crete

Among the various foreign peoples with whom the ancient Egyptians traded were those they called the Keftiu. Today historians know the Keftiu as the Minoans, the inhabitants of the

MINOAN FRESCOES AND BLUE MONKEYS

A number of beautiful frescoes were found in the ruins of the Minoan palace-centers on Crete. However, these wall paintings were not unique to the palaces. Archaeologists discovered several more in private Minoan houses, among them one so alive with murals that excavators dubbed it the "House of the Frescoes" (located northwest of the palace-center at Knossos, in northern Crete). In the second volume of his *Palace of Minos*, the discoverer of the Knossos palace, Britain's Arthur Evans, provided a description of these paintings, saying in part, "The painted decoration of the walls is unrivaled of its kind for its picturesque setting, and the many-colored effect is enhanced, not only by the varied choice of flowers, but the convention of the rocks cut like agates to show their brilliant veins." Of particular note in the House of the Frescoes is one that shows a frolicking blue monkey. Blue monkeys were apparently well-liked by the Minoans because frescoes depicting them have been found in the ruins of several other Minoan structures.

Arthur Evans. *The Palace of Minos at Knossos*. Vol. 2. London: Macmillan, 1921–1936, pp. 466–467.

A painting of a blue monkey from the palace of Minos in Crete.

large Greek island of Crete in the second millennium B.C. (between 2000 and 1000 B.C.). This era of Greek history was part of its Bronze Age, so named because people used tools and weapons made of bronze (an alloy of copper and tin). Named after Minos, a mythical Cretan king, the Minoans ruled Crete until the 1400s B.C.

At that time they had by far the most advanced civilization not only in Greece, but in all of Europe. They erected enormous palace-centers at Knossos (NOS-us) and other locales across Crete, structures that served both as homes for their kings and distribution centers for their prosperous agricultural economy. The highly impressive surviving sections of these buildings show that they were equipped with bathrooms with tubs, running water, and flush toilets.

The Minoans also created dynamic, frequently charming and beautiful art. At first, they borrowed several of their artistic ideas and styles from the Middle East, especially Egypt. In the words of an authority on ancient Greek art, early and even some later Minoan paintings "display the familiar Egyptian side view with the frontal eye, as well as the sharp outlines in solid color."[12] Nevertheless, such similarities between the two artistic traditions were few and of minor consequence. Although the Minoans did absorb some Egyptian artistic concepts, they reinvented them and applied them in fresh ways to fit their own society.

In fact, Minoan painting styles were quite distinctive and executed in a vigorous, lively manner. They express a "love of life" in "bright colors," noted archaeologist William R. Biers writes. He adds that these pictures are fairly "naturalistic," or realistic, and yet "the artist was not afraid of changing colors or distorting natural shapes in order to convey feeling or emotion." Many of the paintings display "a quick, sketchy technique that forced the artist to concentrate on the particular parts of the picture that were most important to him."[13]

The subjects of these Minoan paintings vary considerably. They include scenes from nature showing trees, flowers, land animals, and frequently fish, octopi, and other sea creatures;

views of royal court life and religious rituals, among them sacred dancing; and public sporting events and celebrations.

The most famous genre of Minoan painting is the one showing scenes of what the Greeks called *taurokathapsia*, or bull leaping. The pictures portray agile young athletes of both genders vaulting over the backs of giant bulls, animals that the people of Crete viewed as sacred. The finest surviving example of a bull-leaping painting is the *Toreador Fresco*, found at Knossos. It shows three figures, two girls and a boy, interacting with the bull, each in a different phase of the grand bull leap. "The girl

A Minoan fresco depicts two girls and a boy engaged in bull leaping, an event connected somehow with religion.

on the left is taking hold of the bull's horns in preparation to leap," art historian Wendy Beckett remarks. "The man is in mid-vault [and] the girl on the right has landed and steadies herself with arms outstretched, like a modern gymnast."[14]

The painting is a fresco, as its title reflects. Frescoes were, in fact, the chief form of Minoan painting. The fresco technique involves painting on wet plaster, in contrast to the secco method in which the paint is applied to a dry surface. According to scholar Thomas Sakoulas,

> Painting on wet plaster allowed the pigments of metal and mineral oxides to bind well to the wall, while it required quick execution. The nature of this technique allowed for a high degree of improvisation [invention] and spontaneity [quick thinking] and introduced the element of chance into the final art. Since they had to work within the time constrains of the drying plaster, the painters had to be very skillful, and their fluid brush strokes translated into the graceful outlines that characterize Minoan painting. For this reason, the [fresco] method of painting was most appropriate for the fluid moments of life and nature scenes that the Minoans favored, which contrasted sharply with the strict [conventions] and stereotyping typical of frescoes from other Mediterranean cultures of the same time.[15]

The Minoans were not the only European people for whom the fresco approach to painting would prove highly flexible, effective, and popular. Indeed, frescoes were destined to be employed repeatedly in later Western art. Secco would be used, too, and to great effect, in the next two major world painting traditions—those of Greece and Rome.

2

Greece and Rome: Inventing Styles for the Ages

The lovely, colorful paintings produced in Minoan Crete more than three thousand years ago are today little more than fleeting snapshots of a long-vanished culture. In the 1400s B.C. the Minoans were conquered by the Mycenaeans, a less-cultured folk who dwelled on the Greek mainland. The invaders took over Crete's small empire centered in the southern Greek islands, as well as the Minoans' eastern Mediterranean trading network. The regime change in Crete was noted by the Egyptians and recorded in their wall paintings. The Egyptians still referred to the new merchants who arrived from that distant island as Keftiu. But they dressed slightly differently than those who had come before, and Egyptian painters were careful to depict those minor changes in attire.

Despite their military and economic successes, the Mycenaeans' moment in the sun, so to speak, was brief. Shortly after 1200 B.C. a tremendous catastrophe struck not only Greek civilization but also large sections of the nearby Middle East. Historians still debate the causes. But the present consensus is that waves of attackers from southeastern Europe spread southward and overwhelmed large swaths of territory. The result in the Greek lands was the sudden onset of a dark age in which large-scale building, record-keeping, literacy, and the arts were almost

A thirteenth-century B.C. Mycenaean fresco depicts two people riding in a chariot.

entirely lost. As the poverty-stricken survivors steadily forgot their own heritage, the once strong and vibrant Minoan-Mycenaean world faded into the misty realm of myth.

Greek civilization was not extinct, however, but merely dormant, like a caterpillar in its cocoon, waiting to emerge as a butterfly. When the long dark age finally ended in about 800 B.C., the culture again slowly spread its wings and in the process created a magnificent new civilization. That splendid culture, often called "Classical Greece," created a host of artists whose works awed and thrilled later generations. "Future ages will wonder at us," the fifth-century B.C. Athenian leader Pericles predicted, "as the present age wonders at us now."[16]

This statement was first proven true about three centuries later, after the Romans conquered the Greek lands. Though they viewed the Greeks as politically inferior, the Romans recognized Greek literary and artistic genius and sought to emulate it. Roman artists carried on the traditions established by the Greeks. Later ages came to call the Greco-Roman artistic and cultural fusion "classical" civilization. Artists in those later ages, especially the European Renaissance, were profoundly influenced by the styles and subjects of classical art, including painting.

The Bold, Inquisitive Greeks

Among the gifted Greek artists the Romans greatly admired were painters. The earliest Greek painters were, as the Minoans had been, influenced by Egyptian painting styles. But this rapidly changed. Something was very different about the

The Pitsa Tablet is one of the few surviving examples of ancient Greek painting. It consists of a painted scene on a wooden plaque.

Greeks' outlook on life that made them more inquisitive, bold, and open to change and experimentation than other peoples of their time. As Roy Bolton explains it,

> The Greeks were taking risks. They questioned ideas of philosophy, democracy, art, and science in what looks like a modern way to us now. They had learned from the Egyptians, but they took what they needed from them and founded Western civilization with their new ideas. For the first time painting emerged where scenes were painted with something like reality in mind, not unquestioned tradition. . . . These Greek painters (and their Roman followers who carried on their work) attained incredible levels of skill, which were unsurpassed anywhere until the Renaissance.[11]

In spite of ancient Greek painting's ultimate historical achievement, the earliest Greek painters did not start out producing masterpieces. As has happened in every world painting tradition, the first works created were fairly simple and rudimentary. Most examples of early Classical Greek painting have not survived. One that has gives some idea of the overall style and approach that painters then employed. Dating from about 540 B.C., it consists of a painted scene on a wooden plaque found at Pitsa, in south-central Greece. In the scene, several adults and children march in solemn procession on their way to sacrifice a sheep. The artist first drew the figures as line-drawings and then, as modern cartoonists do, filled in the appropriate spaces with solid colors. Although the picture is attractive, it lacks detail, shading, perspective (to show depth), and other elements of more realistic painting.

Another important surviving example of early Classical Greek painting also displays a simplistic, colorful cartoon-like style. Found in the ruins of the ancient Greek city of Paestum, in southern Italy, and dating from roughly 480 B.C., it consists of a series of pleasant scenes painted on the lid and inside walls of a large stone burial chamber. It is often called the Tomb of the Diver because the painting on the lid shows a young man diving

THE PAINTING BEHIND THE CURTAIN?

In the fourth century B.C., Greek painters achieved a level of realism in their works that would remain unmatched until the advent of Europe's Renaissance many centuries later. A likely exaggerated or possibly even fabricated story connected to the realistic qualities of these ancient paintings has survived. The chief characters are the great painters, Zeuxis and Parrhasios (pa-RAY-shi-us). After each had bragged about his own abilities, the two men decided to stage a competition to see which could paint more realistically than the other. When the time came to compare paintings, Zeuxis produced one that showed a cluster of grapes. Parrhasios admitted that they looked surprisingly real. Indeed, Zeuxis said, they looked so much like the real thing that they had attracted the attention of some birds. Then it was time for Parrhasios to display his own entry in the contest. The two artists walked to his house and entered, after which he told Zeuxis that the painting was behind the curtain on the far side of the room. The eager Zeuxis reached out to draw back the curtain and to his astonishment realized he was touching a painting of a curtain. At that point, there was no doubt in his mind that he had lost the competition to the wily and talented Parrhasios.

from a stone platform into a pond or river. The scenes on the insides of the stone slabs depict a symposium, a party in which Greek men drank wine, listened to music, and told stories.

Toward Visual Realism

Greek painters quickly built on and significantly surpassed this basic approach to their craft, however. Beginning in the fifth century B.C., each succeeding generation produced a group of inventive artists who significantly advanced the genre of painting. Little by little, they left behind the cartoon-like style and moved toward achieving visual realism, each innovator influencing those who came later.

The first so-called master Greek painter, and to this day one of the most famous, was Polygnotus (pa-lig-NOH-tis). He worked in Athens from about 480 to 450 B.C., when the great political leader Pericles was a young man. Polygnotus's

In addition to mural painters, there were Greek artists who applied their talents to rendering figures and scenes on urns, bowls, cups, jars, and other ceramic containers.

best-known work was a mural, or wall-painting, called *The Capture of Troy*. This important painting did not survive the ravages of time, nor did any other large Classical Greek paintings. For that reason, to estimate how many of these works were done in fresco and how many in secco is difficult. Art historians speculate that a majority were frescoes but that the artists often made touch-ups and additions in secco after the surface had dried.

Fortunately for later ages, a few surviving ancient literary accounts describe some of these lost works, providing an idea of what they looked like. The well-known guide book by the second-century A.D. Greek traveler Pausanias, for example, says that Polygnotus's painting of Troy showed several famous characters and scenes from the legendary Trojan War. Among the characters was Helen, the mythical Spartan queen who supposedly ran away with the Trojan prince Paris, setting the conflict in motion.

In this and other paintings, Polygnotus employed a new technique that other Greek artists immediately adopted. Before his time, painters had no concept of how to show depth or perspective, that is, to make some people and objects look farther away than others. To achieve this illusion, Polygnotus placed his figures at different levels across the painting. He scattered "them about at various points in space, instead of confining them to a single ground line as had previously been done," scholar Robert B. Kebric explains. "Landscape figures such as trees and rocks gave an additional feeling of depth. Also, an emotional quality appears to have characterized his work, with figures reacting to what has just happened or what is about to happen."[18]

A more realistic way of showing depth in a painting was introduced by another Classical Greek master, the somewhat younger Agatharchus (ag-uh-THAR-kus). It appears that he first used his approach for indicating perspective in the creation of background paintings for theatrical plays. The first-century B.C. Roman architect Vitruvius, who wrote about the Greek arts in a book that has survived, claimed that Agatharchus discovered how to use a "fixed center." From it, Vitruvius said, lines of sight project outward and "can seem to recede in one part" of a painting "and move closer"[19] in another.

Modern experts think that the "fixed center" Vitruvius spoke of was a vanishing point, a spot in a painting or drawing at which sight lines from the foreground come together in the background. Placing various objects along those sight lines is what creates proper perspective and the illusion of depth. The consensus of the experts is that Agatharchus used two or more vanishing points, rather than one, and depicting true, or proper, perspective requires using one vanishing point. Still, his method made his paintings look considerably more realistic than those of Polygnotus.

Another technical advance the Greeks made in the art of painting was the development of shading, the increasing or decreasing lightness or darkness on painted bodies or objects to give the illusion of three-dimensions. The painted figures in the Tomb of the Diver, like those on Greek vases, were flat-looking because the artist used a single color for their bodies and made no effort to indicate their natural contours. Adding shading to human figures and natural objects alike created a contoured look that increased the level of realism. Ancient sources credit the late fifth-century B.C. Athenian painter Apollodorus (a-pa-luh-DOR-us) with that important breakthrough.

Greek Painting's Zenith

Following these and other technical advances, Greek painting entered its greatest era—the fourth century B.C. One of the leading artists of the period was Zeuxis (ZOOK-sis), who hailed from Heraclea, a Greek city in southern Italy. Ancient writers told how he became extremely wealthy from the numerous commissions he received to paint pictures for both cities and private individuals.

Unfortunately for posterity, none of Zeuxis's works have survived. But some of these reportedly stunning paintings were described by ancient writers. The second-century A.D. Greek author Lucian of Samosata recorded most of the details of

Zeuxis's renowned mural depicting a group of centaurs, mythical creatures with a human upper body and horse-like lower body. The passage says in part,

> On fresh green [grass] appears the mother Centaur, the whole equine part of her stretched on the ground, her hoofs extended backwards; the human part is slightly raised on the elbows. The fore feet are not extended like the others. . . . One of them is bent as in the act of kneeling, with the hoof tucked in, while the other is beginning to straighten and take a hold on the ground —the action of a horse rising. Of the cubs she is holding, one is in her arms suckling in the human fashion, while the other is drawing at the mare's [nipple] like a foal.[20]

Even greater than Zeuxis, the ancient sources claim, was his much younger contemporary Apelles (uh-PEL-eez). The latter was said to have painted portraits of several kings and other leading political movers and shakers. Among them were the successful Macedonian military general King Philip II and his famous son Alexander, later called "the Great." Apelles also did a portrait of one of Alexander's most notorious generals, Antigonus the One-Eyed. In a diplomatic move, the artist hid the self-conscious Antigonus's obvious physical defect in a clever way. "He drew the portrait in three-quarters view," one ancient writer said. That way, "the missing eye would not appear in the picture."[21]

Although Polygnotus, Apollodorus, Zeuxis, Apelles, and the other major Greek painting pioneers were all men, some Greek women made their marks as painters, too. One of the greatest of these female artists lived in the Greek-ruled city of Alexandria, Egypt, in the late fourth century. The daughter of a well-known painter, Timon, her name was Helena. One of Helena's most famous works was called the Battle of Issus. Like Helena, most, if not all of the Greek women painters were daughters of successful male painters who either had no sons or felt comfortable passing on their knowledge of the craft to their daughters. Other

HELENA OF ALEXANDRIA

A number of women painters are mentioned in the surviving works of ancient writers. Among the best, they say was Helena of Alexandria, who lived and worked in that Egyptian city in the late 300s B.C., not long after it had been established by the Macedonian Greek conqueror Alexander III (later called "the Great"). Little is known about her life and works, but there seems little doubt that she was the daughter of the popular Greek painter Timon, who seems to have taught her everything he knew about his trade. Some ancient sources claim that Helena had an interest in portraying historical events, including battle scenes. In fact, she was credited by a few with a famous painting depicting Alexander charging at the Persian king Darius III in the midst of the battle of Issus (333 B.C.). One source said that more than three centuries later someone bought the painting and took it to Rome. There, it went on display in one of that city's town squares. The work no longer exists. But a mosaic found in the ruins of Pompeii, the Italian city buried by a volcanic eruption in A.D. 79, may have been based on it.

This famous Roman mosaic of the battle of Issus is thought to be a copy of Helena's original painting done three hundred years before.

well-known Greek women painters included Timarete (or Thamyris), Eirene, Kalypso, and Olympias.

Rome Carries On the Greek Tradition

Some Greek painters, both men and women, lived in Greece's Roman period. Lasting from about 30 B.C. to A.D. 476, this was the long era in which all of the formerly independent Greek-inhabited lands in the Mediterranean were ruled by Rome, which had conquered them. The Romans held the Greek arts, including painting, in high esteem and readily copied Greek artistic methods, styles, and even subjects. Moreover, although a number of Romans became painters, large numbers of paintings produced in the Roman Empire were

A Roman fresco in a home in Pompeii. Roman frescoes often covered entire walls from floor to ceiling and depicted scenes from everyday life, myth, and religion.

done by Greeks who lived in that realm. Thus, the Roman painting tradition was in large degree a continuation of the Greek one.

A fair number of large Roman paintings, especially those on walls, have survived. The majority were executed in fresco. Artists in the Roman period, like those in the prior Greek eras, used pigments made from natural materials, especially minerals and animal and vegetable dyes. For instance, red pigment came from either iron oxide or cinnabar (mercury sulfide). White came from chalk, marble dust, or oyster shells. A painter first heated these substances to dry them, then ground them into powders and mixed them with liquids such as water, honey, or raw egg, along with animal glues to make the paint stick well to the plastered wall. When a fresco was finished, the artist applied a layer of transparent glue or wax to give it a glossy, fairly durable surface.

Modern art experts learned about these ancient paints and techniques in part by studying the surviving Roman murals. Of those that are largely intact and in the best shape, most were discovered in the ruins of Pompeii and Herculaneum. These were the two largest of several small towns buried in the great A.D. 79 eruption of the volcano Mt. Vesuvius, lying near the Bay of Naples in western Italy.

These impressive and in some cases strikingly sophisticated and beautiful paintings show that Roman painters, and the Greeks they emulated, had mastered shading, basic perspective, and other elements of realism. Also, many of the paintings in the buried cities were not created merely as added decoration in homes. Instead, they also substituted for what people today would call home furnishings. Often covering entire walls from floor to ceiling, they depicted life-size images of chairs and other furniture, windows and doors, and so forth. Art historian Richard Zuccarini writes,

> In Pompeii and Herculaneum, "fortuitously" preserved for us by layers of volcanic ash, we can see how fresco was used to brighten windowless stone rooms. The Romans painted scenes of the outdoors, lively people, and . . .

doors, arches, and windows to help relieve claustrophobia. . . . In some houses there is found layer-upon-layer of lime plaster [each of which once held a fresco], indicating that wall paintings may have been changed [often], much as we change wallpaper.[22]

Roman Painting Subjects

In addition to huge murals that imitated home furnishings, Roman painters turned out works of all sizes, types, and subjects. Some were portable works, done on wood panels, which a family could carry with them when they moved to a new home. Subjects included landscapes, including gardens, a favorite theme among Romans; mythological scenes; and still lifes (paintings of groups of commonplace inanimate objects).

The Romans also had a particular interest in painting portraits. Roman portraits tended to be extremely naturalistic and frank. That is, they portrayed people exactly as they were, including any wrinkles, moles, warts, or other imperfections. One of the finest surviving Roman painted portraits was found in a house in Pompeii. Done in fresco sometime in the first century A.D., it depicts a well-to-do baker, Terentius Neo, and his wife.

In addition, Roman painters worked in two genres that were quite specific to Roman culture. One, the "triumphal painting," was displayed in the triumph, or victory parade, given for a Roman military general after winning a major battle. Triumphal paintings often depicted key moments from battles or other important aspects of the general's campaign. The first-century A.D. Jewish historian Josephus wrote, "The art and marvelous craftsmanship of these [paintings] revealed the incidents [of the campaign] to those who had not seen them happen as clearly as if they had been there."[23] The other typically Roman painting subject was the gladiator. Fights in which gladiators fought to the death were wildly popular throughout most of the years of the Empire. Painted portraits of these warriors were no less fashionable and decorated town squares across the realm.

PORTRAIT OF A TROUBLED MARRIAGE?

Art historian Wendy Beckett provides this thoughtful description of the fresco portrait of the baker Terentius Neo and his wife from Pompeii, a work that survived nearly intact because it was entombed in volcanic materials in the eruption of Mt. Vesuvius.

The portrait remains essentially Roman, with all the interest concentrated on their personalities. The husband, a slightly uncouth, gawky, earnest young man, looks at the viewer with anxious appeal, while the wife looks away into the distance, musing [thinking] and holding her writing stylus to her delicately pointed chin. Both seem lonely, as if their differently directed gazes reveal something of their marriage. They live together, but they do not share their lives, and there is an added poignancy [emotional aspect]. The house of Neo . . . was still unfinished at the time of the eruption, so it is possible that this lonely marriage was of tragically short duration.

Wendy Beckett. *The Story of Painting*. New York: Dorling Kindersley, 2000, p. 30.

A portrait of baker Terentius Neo and his wife was excavated at Pompeii.

A Roman wall fresco depicts a garden scene complete with monuments and birds. The Romans liked to put outdoor scenes on their walls.

Passages from Roman literature indicate that most Romans, like most people today, expected their way of life and civilization, including their arts, to last forever. But as all civilizations inevitably do, Rome's eventually disintegrated. Invasions by tribal peoples from central and northern Europe weakened Rome's empire. In the fifth and sixth centuries Rome's rule gave way to a medieval European culture that was initially far less organized and less advanced than Roman civilization. Among other artistic traditions, painting suffered serious reversals and almost disappeared. As they had in the distant past, important aspects of culture went into a kind of cocoon, waiting to be reborn in a different time and place.

Beyond the West: Masterworks Across the Globe

The Romans viewed their mighty dominion as occupying the very center of the world. They knew that other lands existed beyond the Empire. But they saw them as second-rate and marginal, occupying the less important edges of civilization and therefore lacking in the kinds of cultural refinements Rome enjoyed. Historians now know that this outlook was sorely short-sighted and mistaken. At the Roman Empire's height of power in the second century A.D., China's painting tradition was already many centuries old. At the time, and in the centuries to come, the best Chinese artists regularly turned out what are now viewed as masterworks. Further south, India had its own ancient painting tradition. Meanwhile, on the opposite side of the globe, in Mesoamerica (ancient Mexico and Central America), Maya artists created magnificent murals. Some examples survive with their rich array of colors still vibrant.

These represent only a few of many far-flung early non-Western painting traditions, which also include those in early Japan and Africa. None became as long-lived and widely influential as that of the West, centered in Europe. Nevertheless, each produced at least a few artists, most of whose names are now forgotten, with talent rivaling the greatest European masters.

India's Lush Rock Paintings

The works of many, though by no means all, of these non-Western artists were inspired by their religious faith. This was certainly the case with early Indian painters. Like Europe and southern Africa, India has ancient caves in which members of prehistoric societies painted images on the rock walls. The Indian versions, dating as far back as 5500 B.C. or somewhat earlier, are not nearly as old as those in Europe (some of which are more than thirty thousand years old). Yet they are no less vivid and impressive than those in France and Spain. Rock paintings found in the Bhimbetka caves, in north-central India, contain images of humans involved in various religious rites, as well as in hunting animals. (Interestingly, one shows a beast stalking a person.) Some of the original colors—mainly red and white, with lesser amounts of green and yellow—are still surprisingly bright.

Rock paintings found in caves in India date as far back as 5500 B.C. and are no less impressive than their Western counterparts.

As outside groups periodically entered India from the west over the millennia that followed, some developed individual painting traditions. One of the finest and longest-lasting was the one that produced thousands of images on cave walls at Ajanta, in Maharashtra (in west-central India), between the first century B.C. and fifth century A.D. A large portion of these finely made, frequently lush artworks were inspired by the Buddhist faith, which originated in India in the 400s B.C. Executed with the fresco technique, many depict the Buddha himself in legendary scenes from his life.

A well-known and beautifully rendered example of the Buddhist paintings at Ajanta is often called *Court Life Scene*. It shows the young Buddha, when he was still the Indian prince Siddhartha, climbing into his wife's bed and informing her that he plans to become a poor monk and seek the meaning of life. In the words of a modern art historian,

> The female figure [is] particularly graceful and delicate. Her face is in the center of the scene and . . . the grace and light coloration of her presence serves to intensify the figure of the prince, whose limbs, body, and head seem to envelop and protect her. . . . Both [figures] are depicted with great vigor. The woman, wearing a dress of fine material, leans delicately against the body of her husband. Her attitude suggests confidence in her powers of seduction. [Siddhartha's] body is athletic and firmly structured. Rich ornamentation [decoration] indicates the rank of the prince and reminds us of the luxurious worldly pleasures that he will now have the strength to leave behind.[24]

China's Distinctive Styles

To the north of India, in China, the first substantial painting tradition emerged in the so-called Warring States Era, lasting from the early 400s to the 220s B.C. Some of the images were painted on silk, but most were done on the stone or brick walls lining tombs. Scenes from the royal court, everyday life, and myths predominated. Even at this early stage, Chinese artists displayed an overall approach, perhaps best described as delicate and thoughtful, that long remained distinctive among the world's painting styles. Indeed, Roy Bolton explains, the Chinese

> developed a rather different approach to painting from that of the Romanized West. Calligraphy [the art of elaborate lettering] was as prized as painting, even more so at times, so the painting traditions that grew up [in China] relied on well-defined ink outlines. The purpose of painting was very different, too. It was less dominated by religious imagery, and was practiced for a small, educated elite of nobles and bureaucrats. In landscape painting it was tied to meditation.[25]

The Chinese use of ink outlines, sometimes filled in with color (most often pastels rather than bright hues), was dependent on a substance made by mixing carbon black or lampblack with animal glues. Although long called India ink, most experts think it originated in China. According to Hans L.C. Jaffe, "India ink, with its all-inclusive range from palest gray to deepest black, contains within itself all the colors of the world. India ink painting is one of the chief glories of Far Eastern art, and . . . [it was] with a new concern for light and atmosphere that [it] made its most universal impact."[26]

In part because of the unique technical and visual qualities of ink painting, Chinese art came into its own with the emergence of landscape painting in the 400s and 500s A.D. For centuries to come, the typical style featured a light pastel or nearly colorless monochrome tone with intricate ink lines and curves depicting complex pastoral scenes. These scenes were littered with knobby peaks, gnarled trees, winding streams, and solitary Buddhist temples nestled in quiet groves. Early masters of the style included Wang Wei (born 699) and Jing Hao (circa 870).

Those distinctive Chinese landscapes became more realistic over time, and the zenith of realism in the genre occurred during the northern Song dynasty (A.D. 960–1127). Among the talented painters of this period whose works have survived are Fan Kuan (circa 960), Xu Xi (circa 1020), Guo Xi (circa

Chinese landscape paintings advanced during the northern Song dynasty. This landscape by Fan Kuan is indicative of the style of the period.

THE FOUR GREAT MING MASTERS

Ancient China turned out numerous talented painters over the centuries. In particular, the period of the Ming dynasty (1368–1644) was a golden age for artists. Art historian Hans L.C. Jaffe here briefly describes what modern experts call the four great masters of the era, Shen Chou, Wen Cheng-Ming, T'ang Yin, and Ch'iu Ying.

These men merit as high a place in world art as their Western contemporaries, Leonardo [and] Michelangelo. [Shen Chou's] soft colors tone down the ruggedness of the [countryside he painted] and the tiny figures he introduces lend a human dimension to an awesome landscape. Wen Cheng-Ming, Shen Chou's friend and pupil, was subtler and more sensitive in both brushwork and color. . . . T'ang Yin's was the most unbridled [outgoing] personality of the group, and he painted not only landscapes, but also remarkably fine [human] figures. [He] passed his days in the company of beautiful women. (It was said of him that he would paint a picture merely for a cup of wine.). The youngest of the circle, Ch'iu Ying, was the only one not from a well-to-do family. . . . His figures and landscapes are executed with delicate brushwork, though his colors tend to be vivid.

Hans L.C. Jaffe. *The History of World Painting*. London: New Orchard Editions, 1985, p. 367.

Chinese Ming artist T'ang Yin painted this landscape in the late fifteenth century.

1020), and Mi Fu (1051). Their tradition was carried forth in the southern Song period (1127–1279) by Xia Gui (late 1100s), Qian Xuan (1235), and others. Qian's works are distinguished by their use of brighter colors, especially green and blue, than those of most other Chinese landscape painters.

Chinese Influences on Japan

In addition to their intrinsic worth as fine art, the paintings of the early Chinese masters exerted a strong influence on artists in neighboring lands.

This influence was particularly profound in traditional (ancient) Japan. When Buddhism (which the Chinese had earlier adopted from India) spread from China to Japan in the seventh and eighth centuries, Chinese painting styles and methods transferred along with it. Accordingly, many of the early Japanese versions of Chinese works portrayed scenes from Buddha's life and/or mythical beings associated with Buddhism. Some of the finest examples were painted on the walls of the magnificent "Golden Hall" of the Horyuji Temple (the oldest surviving wooden structure in the world), a few miles south of Nara, in southern Japan. Tragically, nearly all of these masterworks were destroyed in a fire in January 1949. But photos of them fortunately preserve their appearance.

A more native, or national, style of Japanese painting—known as Yamato-e—began to replace the borrowed Chinese motifs in the Hein period (A.D. 794–1185). The name derives from Yamato, the region of southern Japan where it began, and the word *e*, meaning "painting" in Japanese. It was not completely original, as it was inspired by early Chinese landscapes. However, it quickly developed its own distinct look and feel. Most works in the genre depict softly rolling hills, the change of seasons, and other aspects of quiet nature. Japanese artists painted them on doors, folding screens (then found in most Japanese houses), and handscrolls.

These scrolls, called in Japanese, *emakimono*, or *emaki* for short, were rolls of paper on which historical or fictional stories were written. *Emaki* paintings illustrated the stories. The

This painting illustrates the text of a Japanese *emakimono*, or painted scroll, describing an attack on Sanjo Palace.

most famous examples are the striking images created for the *Tales of Genji*, a renowned Japanese literary work, dating from circa 1130.

Later, in Japan's Muromachi period (1333–1573), Japanese painters once more came under the sway of Chinese art. This time they adopted the monochromatic ink-painting style that had reached its height during China's Song dynasty in the 900s to 1200s. It was while this style of painting was popular in Japan that Western merchants first began visiting the country.

African Body Painting

Unlike early Japan, early African cultures (not including Egypt) experienced few outside artistic influences. This may be one reason that no major conventional painting traditions developed in Africa until early modern times. Although prehistoric artists painted thousands of pictures on the walls of caves across southern Africa, over time most native African cultures seem to have lost interest in two-dimensional art. Instead, several African societies experimented with the three-dimensional medium of sculpture. In some places, notably what is now Nigeria, artists produced highly sophisticated and stunningly beautiful figurines, busts, and other sculpted images.

In the meantime, some African societies retained the two-dimensional art in the very ancient but less permanent form of body-painting. Worn for religious rituals, family celebrations, and other important social activities, these paintings were often highly intricate and detailed and required long hours or even days to apply. The paints were made from various plant saps and oils, clays, ash, and other natural materials. Although the hues were often traditional tribal colors, they were sometimes selected to make a personal statement. Designs ranged from geometric shapes to complex swirls or patterns of dots.

A considerable amount is known about this singular kind of painting because a number of African groups still practice it. Among them are the Dinka and Nuba in southern Sudan; Berber women in the Atlas Mountains (in northwestern Africa), who paint their faces prior to annual courtship rituals; and various groups in Chad, Zaire, Ethiopia, and Nigeria. All say that their body-painting techniques date back many centuries, in some cases possibly thousands of years.

The art appears particularly old among the people of the Surma and Mursi tribes in Ethiopia's Omo Valley, near the border with Kenya. They regularly paint their faces and/or bodies with pigments made from stone dust mixed with water and view the practice as a formal kind of art. In fact, according to the book *Ethiopia: Peoples of the Omo Valley* by German photographer Hans Silvester, who studied and documented the tribes in person, among the art forms practiced in the region they rank it higher than sculpture, music, and dance.

Mesoamerica's "Sistine Chapel"

Other ancient peoples who used body-painting dwelled on the opposite side of the Atlantic Ocean from Africa. Various Mesoamerican tribes and groups decorated their bodies, including the Maya, although the latter practiced more conventional forms of painting, too. The Maya fashioned miniature scenes on pottery, like the ancient Greeks did, and painted their temples red and white. (The pigments have disappeared over time due to weathering and erosion, leaving the buildings' outer surfaces plain and drab.)

The main painting venue for the Maya, however, was the mural, at which they excelled. To make their paints, they mixed vegetable dyes and powdered minerals with various liquids, managing to create a wide range of colors. Their most stunning and famous one, made from plant leaves and local clays, has come to be called "Maya blue" by modern art historians. Maya artists applied these colors liberally and in bright hues, as the ancient Minoans of Crete did.

Regrettably, a majority of the original Maya murals have disappeared due to the humid climate in Central America. Of the few that have survived, some of the best-preserved are those at Bonampak, in Chiapas, Mexico, dating from around A.D. 790. They contain scenes of nobles in elaborate formal outfits, battles, and religious sacrifices.

Another group of intact Maya murals was found in 2001 in San Bartolo, in Guatemala. Dating from circa A.D. 100, the paintings are in a specially constructed chamber beneath a stone pyramid, protected from the elements, which partially explains why they have survived. Excavators were stunned by the intricacy and beauty of the murals, which depict mythological events, including the Maya creation story. Some observers have called them the "Sistine Chapel of Maya art" (a reference to the splendid paintings done by Michelangelo on the ceiling of the Sistine Chapel, in Rome, during the Renaissance). William Saturno of Harvard University's Peabody Museum of Archaeology, who leads the ongoing digs, writes,

The paintings at Bonampak are some of the best of the surviving Maya murals. Scenes of nobles, battles, and religious sacrifices adorn the walls and ceilings of this so-called Maya Sistine Chapel.

In Western terms, it's like knowing only modern art and then stumbling on a Michelangelo or a Leonardo. [The murals demonstrate] that early Maya painting had achieved a high level of sophistication and grace.... The artistic and physical evidence of the Maya's earliest kings revealed at San Bartolo is among the most important finds in Maya archaeology in the last few decades. It has opened a window into the very origins of Maya civilization. As we excavate the site further and piece together more images and glyphs [picture-writing] from the mural fragments we have discovered, new surprises could be revealed.[27]

MAKING MAYA BLUE

One striking aspect of ancient Maya painting is the extremely vivid blue paint employed, which modern investigators came to call "Maya blue." In this passage from the extensive and useful articles on their website, two experts on Maya civilization explain how the color was made.

The ancient Maya combined skills in organic chemistry and mineralogy to create an important technology—the first permanent organic pigment. The unique color and stability of Maya Blue, the most durable Maya color, [has] only recently has been reproduced. The Maya blue pigment is a composite of organic [living] and inorganic [nonliving] constituents, primarily indigo dyes derived from the leaves of añil plants combined with palygorskite (Sepiolite), a natural clay. [It is the cooking of this mixture] at 100° C that makes it turn from blackish to its exquisite [blue]

tone. Smaller trace amounts of other mineral additives have also been identified. Due to its attractive turquoise color and light fastness [ability to maintain its color], Maya blue was widely used in mural paintings, sculptures, ceramics, and codices [books].

AuthenticMaya.com. "Maya Art." www.authenticmaya.com/maya_art.htm.

Maya blue pigment was a composite of organic and inorganic materials mixed together with clay.

The art treasures found at San Bartolo, as well as surviving paintings from India, China, Japan, and elsewhere, provide mute testimony of an important truth. They show that the West was not the world's only civilized area that could and did produce masterworks of the painter's art. Indeed, no region, nation, or people has or likely will ever own a monopoly on artistic talent.

Europe's Renaissance: The Zenith of Realism

Of all the periods, eras, or movements of painting in world history, perhaps none is more renowned and admired than that of Europe's Renaissance, which lasted from about 1400 to 1600. This great artistic period was the outcome of educated Europeans rediscovering the classical arts of ancient Greece and Rome, including architecture, sculpture, and painting.

Renaissance artists did not merely copy earlier ideas and methods, however. Rather, they were profoundly inspired by classical arts and used them as stepping stones to the creation of their own distinctive artworks in bold new styles. In the process, they produced some of history's most splendid and memorable paintings. They also set the stage for most Western art to come. "By creating artwork of staggering beauty," art historian Elke Linda Buchholz writes, the great Renaissance artists "became recognized as the model for many generations to come."[28]

The Age of Illustrated Bibles

It must be emphasized that the Renaissance was not an abrupt burst of artistic activity having no immediate precedents and models other than those of long-ago Greece and Rome. Instead, it was the final stage of Europe's long medieval era, which had began with the fall of the western Roman Empire in the fifth and sixth centuries. After Rome's demise, most longstanding traditions and expertise in the arts, including painting, were lost. Thus, during the long pre-Renaissance medieval centuries, major forms of painting "in western Europe had languished," Roy Bolton says. "It was left either to monks to reproduce holy images or artisans to paint simple wall decorations under the direction of their employers."[29]

In fact, for several centuries following Rome's fall the main form of painting in Europe was very small-scale. It consisted almost entirely of illuminated manuscripts. These were illustrations for copies of the Bible and other religious books that were painstakingly produced by hand by monks working in monasteries. The first noteworthy versions of these illustrated holy books appeared in Ireland and Anglo-Saxon England

For several centuries after Rome's fall illuminated manuscripts were the dominant type of painting. Bibles were painstakingly hand written and illustrated.

between about 650 and 800. The colorful, decorative images usually consisted of carefully rendered abstract designs, along with plant stems and leaves, and a few animals and human faces.

More complex paintings for illuminated manuscripts developed under the Carolingians, the family line of rulers, among them the famous Charlemagne, that controlled much of Europe between 783 and 900. Sponsored by these rulers, monks and nuns in France and Germany crafted both full Bibles and separate sets of the Gospels (the first four books of the New Testament). The images decorating these volumes now included full human forms sitting or walking through rooms in houses, gardens, and other picturesque settings. According to art historian H.W. Janson,

> Almost every monastery had a workshop for making copies of the Bible and other books. This was done by hand because printing had not yet been invented. The monks did not even know about paper, [so] they wrote on vellum, a material made from the skin of calves. . . . For a long time, [the illuminations in these books] were the most important kind of medieval painting.[30]

Romanesque and Gothic Paintings

A larger and more ambitious painting style emerged in Europe in what art historians call the Romanesque period, which started in about 1050. It consisted mainly of murals for the walls of churches. As illuminations for Bibles had been, Romanesque wall paintings were inspired by religious faith, since so much of European medieval life revolved around deeply held Christian beliefs and ceremonies. One modern expert explains,

> Church walls and ceilings were painted extensively, to guide the predominately illiterate churchgoers and serve as a form of devotion. [France's] large Cluniac monastery [originated this style]. Unfortunately, none of its artwork survived, but [murals from] other early French churches suggest [that it looked] dynamic and animated.[31]

The best preserved of the surviving Romanesque religious murals—done in fresco in about 1090—well illustrates this animated look. Located in the church in the town of Saint-Savin sur Gartempe, in western France, it shows crowds of workers busily and diligently raising the Tower of Babel in the famous Bible story. From the large amount of detail, the artist or artists clearly labored long and hard on the mural. Yet the figures are mere cartoons, and the scene contains no perspective or other attempt to indicate depth. "Their liveliness," Hans L.C. Jaffe remarks, "is achieved without any attempt at realism."[32] So European painting was still considerably inferior in technical quality to both the Roman art of the past and the Renaissance art to come.

Some minimal advances in technique occurred in Europe's next pre-Renaissance art period—the Gothic, which began in the late 1100s. Gothic art was noteworthy for the large amount

The abbey church in France's Saint-Savin sur Gartempe was heavily painted with scenes from the Bible to educate illiterate churchgoers.

One of the most important painters of the early Italian Renaissance also had one of the shortest careers of any artist. When he came into the world in 1401 in a village near Florence, his birth name was Tomasso di Ser Giovanni di Simone. However, history knows him simply as Masaccio. This nickname means "clumsy Tom" or "messy Tom" in Italian and perhaps gives a small hint about his personal attributes. After arriving in Florence as a teenager, he avidly studied the works of Giotto and other prior painters. The young Masaccio also became close friends with the architect Filippo Brunelleschi, who seems to have taught him about the recently rediscovered technique of linear perspective. This method gave Masaccio's paintings a feeling of three-dimensionality that the works of most earlier painters lacked. He also became a master of realistically portraying the human figure. His most important paintings were part of a series of frescoes done for Florence's Church of Santa Maria del Carmine in the 1420s, including the renowned *Expulsion of Adam and Eve from Paradise*. Seemingly nearing the height of his career, Masaccio died in 1428 at the age of twenty-seven. The circumstances remain somewhat mysterious, as some accounts said he was poisoned by a rival painter, but this was never proven legally or otherwise. After his untimely passing his works were widely praised and studied by generations of young painters.

Masaccio painted a series of stunning frescoes for Florence's Church of Santa Maria del Carmine in the 1420s.

of painting done on wooden panels of varying thickness. A majority of the major Gothic panel paintings were executed to decorate the interiors of churches, particularly the altars. (Large artworks done for altars are called altarpieces.)

One of the finer examples of this art form is the *Altarpiece of St. Peter*, painted in about 1280 by Guido da Siena. The large panel painting shows St. Peter sitting on a carved wooden throne, surrounded by smaller scenes from his life. Much larger and more famous is the *Maesta Altarpiece*, completed in 1311 in the cathedral in Siena, Italy. The painter, Duccio di Buoninsegna (bwaw-neen-SEN-yah), created a large assembly of interconnected painted panels depicting scenes from the lives of Jesus and his mother, Mary. "The painting is a work of such powerful austerity [solemnity] and grace," Wendy Beckett points out, "that we become conscious of the urgency of its Christian message."[33]

The most important Gothic painter hailed from Florence, in northern Italy, which was fast becoming one of Europe's major cultural centers. His name was Cenni di Pepi, but posterity knows him better by his nickname, Cimabue. Like other panel paintings of the era, Cimabue's had a rather flat and somewhat unnatural look. However, he made some significant advances over all of the medieval painters that preceded him. He employed more realistic skin tones and hefty amounts of gold leaf to symbolize heaven and the divine, for instance. He also injected noticeable feelings of emotion in his subject's faces. Regarding this human aspect of Cimabue's art, Beckett asserts that his great work, the *Maesta*, showing Mary holding the baby Jesus, "has a great sweetness and dignity, surpassing in emotional content the rigid, stylized figures"[34] of the past.

The Door to the Renaissance Opens

The second way that Cimabue advanced the painting art was by teaching and mentoring the man who in a sense opened the door to Renaissance painting. Giotto di Bondone, usually called Giotto for short, was born in a small village north of Florence in

1267. His most important feat was to expand on his teacher's tentative moves toward greater realism in painting. In fact, among the many charming stories about the two men is one in which as a joke the young Giotto painted a fly on one of Cimabue's unfinished paintings. When the older man resumed work on it, he supposedly tried several times to brush the fly away before he realized it wasn't real.

Whether or not this tale is true, after Giotto completed his apprenticeship with Cimabue, he went on to produce a series of stunning works that surpassed even those of his mentor.

To create the impression of depth, Giotto employed methods such as adding extra background detail, simple perspective, and subtle uses of shading.

Giotto used techniques such as shading, simple perspective, and background detail to generate a illusion of depth in his paintings. He was also more successful in portraying human emotions than prior medieval painters. "His bright, original coloring and feeling-filled characters must have seemed like scenes from real life compared to the rigid"[35] figures of his predecessors, one art expert writes. In addition, Giotto's fame and influence became so great that he significantly expanded the social status and stature of painters. As Bolton puts it,

> He almost single-handedly turned the old view of the painter as a simple craftsman on its head. He showed people that a good artist was a master of original, subtle thought. With Giotto came the celebrity cult of the artist. From now on the history of art becomes not just a list of what was painted when, but the history of great artists."[36]

To Giotto's advances, the major European painters who followed him added some other vital new ideas. The most profound was a fresh sense that when Rome fell the world had lost something magical—the Greco-Roman fascination for the intrinsic worth and beauty of human beings. European intellectuals of the 1300s and 1400s came to believe that this focus on humanity, not God and religion, had been the primary inspirational factor of classical art. Moreover, this way of approaching art had been pure, majestic, and was something to be revived and imitated. Buchholz concisely explains the principal motivation of the emerging Renaissance artists:

> Consciously turning away from Gothic ideas, artists and distinguished scholars used the literature and statues of the ancient world as models. The movement initiated a far-reaching change in religious ideas. The center of artistic interest was no longer God, the omnipresent being, but rather humanity. Underlying these changes was an intense striving for a closeness to nature and a renewed desire to depict the beauty of the human figure.[37]

The Italian painter Paolo Uccello (1397–1475) typified other Renaissance painters in his constant efforts to make the objects in his paintings look as realistic as possible. To this end, he spent a great many hours eagerly studying the phenomenon of perspective, attempting to explain it in mathematical terms. In his famous book about the lives of the major Renaissance artists, Italian painter, architect, and historian Giorgio Vasari (1511–1574) recalls a charming story he had heard about Uccello and his wife. Supposedly, she said that her husband frequently stayed up all night in his study, trying to work out the best methods for using vanishing points, the keys to making perspective work. When she called him to come to bed, she claimed, he would often say: "Oh, what a lovely thing this perspective is!"

Quoted in Giorgio Vasari. *Lives of the Painters, Sculptors, and Architects*. Vol. 1. London: Dent, 1963, p. 104.

Aiming Toward Realism

When this new breed of European intellectuals and artists looked at the surviving statues of Greek and Roman times, they were struck by how realistically they rendered the bodies of humans and animals. They assumed that Greek and Roman paintings, none of which had yet been unearthed, had been likewise realistic. (This assumption turned out to be correct.) Moreover, Cimabue, Giotto, and the leading artists who had immediately preceded them had already been moving toward a look of increased naturalism in painting. This trend toward realism therefore became one of the major features of Renaissance painting. One modern historian comments, "The urge to make something that looked absolutely alive seized hold of artists of the Renaissance."[38]

A number of early Renaissance painters contributed to these trends and goals—to achieve realism, to portray the beauty of the human form, and to recapture the visual and intellectual ideals of classical antiquity. Among others, they included Fra Angelico (born circa 1395), who worked mainly in Florence; Paolo Uccello (b. 1397), Florence; Masaccio (Tommaso di Ser Giovanni di Simone, b. 1401), Florence; Giovanni Bellini (b. 1430), Venice; Andrea Mantegna (b. 1431), Rome; and Sandro Botticelli (b. 1445), Florence and Rome. The working places of these early masters call attention to the fact that the Renaissance began and initially flourished in Italy. In addition to Florence, Venice, and Rome, other Italian cities that nurtured communities of painters included Padua, Milan, Pisa, Siena, and Mantua.

It was not long, however, before the Renaissance spread to northern Europe. Northern painters, who also championed realism, humanism, and other Renaissance ideals, began to employ Italian subjects, styles, and techniques in the mid-to-late 1400s. A few of the more important northern Renaissance painters were Jan van Eyck (born circa 1395), who worked in Belgium; Hieronymous Bosch (circa 1450), the Netherlands; Albrecht Dürer (b. 1471), Germany; and Hans Holbein the Younger (b. 1497), Germany and Switzerland.

Of the numerous contributions these various artists made to the painting art, those of Van Eyck and Bellini were of particular importance in the long term. Before the Renaissance, European painters mainly employed a kind of paint called tempera. To make it, they mixed powdered pigments with egg yoke, water or some other liquid, and a small amount of glue to make sure the paint would stick to the painting surface. In late medieval times, however, a few Dutch artists experimented with oil-based paints. It was Van Eyck who perfected the oil-painting medium and showed other painters in northern Europe that the use of oil allowed for the creation of more elaborate detail than did tempera. (Because oil paint took much longer to dry, painters had more time to add detail or make changes.) Soon afterward, Bellini, who had long followed and greatly admired Van Eyck's work, introduced oil paints to Italy. In this way, oil largely and permanently replaced tempera in Europe.

Jan van Eyck's *The Madonna in Church* shows the detail that was made possible by the use of oil paints.

The Three Giants

Bellini, Van Eyck, Botticelli, and the others listed above all produced masterpieces during the Renaissance. But the zenith of painting in the era arrived with the works of three men who came to be seen both as giants of their time and as being among the greatest painters in history. They were Leonardo da Vinci (born 1452), Michelangelo Buonarroti (b. 1475), and Raphael (b. Raphaello Sanzio, 1483).

Among Leonardo's contributions was the perfection of aerial perspective, which added a new dimension of realism to paintings. He observed that the farther away an object is from an observer, the more its color shifts toward a bluish hue. (This is due to the way the atmosphere absorbs and scatters certain components of light over a distance.) Leonardo also noticed that the haziness of the atmosphere increases with distance. In addition, he found that slightly blurring the edges of facial features and objects in his paintings, a technique called sfumato, made them look softer and more naturalistic.

Leonardo applied this knowledge to his paintings with spectacular results. His two greatest works—the *Last Supper* (1497) and the *Mona Lisa* (1506)—both employ them, along with ordinary perspective and other tricks of the trade. Generations of artists and art lovers alike have studied the *Mona Lisa*

Leonardo da Vinci's *Mona Lisa* is one of the most studied paintings in history.

(which today hangs in the Louvre, in Paris), drinking in its elegance and trying to analyze what makes it so compelling, in a sense a painting for the ages. Part of its allure is undoubtedly Leonardo's technical mastery. Yet the work also has a less definable, more mysterious quality about it that seems to be related to the penetrating expression on the subject's face, which appears to hide a multitude of secrets. Perhaps the noted English art critic Walter Pater (born 1839) summarized it best when he said,

> All the thoughts and experience of the world have [been] etched and molded there [in her face]. She is older than the rocks among which she sits. Like the vampire, she has been dead many times, and learned the secrets of the grave; and has been [a] diver in deep seas [of the human imagination].[39]

Surpassing the Ancients

Less mysterious but no less impressive were the paintings of Michelangelo, who was also a superb architect and sculptor. His painting masterpieces were the dozens of huge frescoes he did on the ceiling of the Sistine Chapel, in the Vatican in Rome, between 1508 and 1512. They show a series of scenes from the Old Testament, including the work's grand centerpiece —the so-called "Creation of Adam." It depicts God floating toward Adam, the first human, intent on giving him the spark of life. "No other [artistic] work in the Western world has been so much reproduced, written about, and commented upon,"[40] one writer observes. As Robert Cumming describes it,

> God, the Father, with a stern, gray-bearded face that signals his absolute authority, is surrounded by his angels. He crosses the heavens like a cosmic meteor. Adam, physically perfect in face and limb . . . seems to receive from God's right finger a charge that is beginning to run through his body like electricity, giving him physical and spiritual life. He looks toward God with an expression that embraces many emotions, including wonder and obedience.[41]

THE MYSTERY OF THE SISTINE MADONNA

Raphael's *Sistine Madonna*, completed in about 1513, not long before his death, is widely viewed as one of his greatest works. It was originally commissioned by the monks of the Monastery of San Sisto, in Piacenza (in northwestern Italy) to adorn their altar area. The painting shows Mary standing on a cloud and holding the infant Jesus while Saint Sixtus, Saint Barbara, and some playful cherubs look on. For centuries some observers have remarked about the facial expression the artist gave to the baby Jesus—what has been described as a subtly startled and/or worried look. Some modern art historians have offered an explanation for this mystery. They suggest that Raphael, who was known for his sense of humor, took into consideration the fact that the painting was originally located directly across from a large crucifix. Thus, they say, the artist made it appear that the infant in the picture was in a sense gazing out, with at least a bit of apprehension, at his future suffering on the cross.

Raphael's Sistine Madonna *is considered one of his greatest works. Completed in 1513, it was commissioned by the monks of the monastery of San Sisto in Piacenza, Italy.*

The third great giant of Renaissance painting, Raphael, was in his twenties when the older Michelangelo began work on the Sistine Chapel ceiling in 1508. That year was important for the younger man as well. Mightily influenced by both Leonardo and Michelangelo, along with other recent masters, he had already become widely renowned and beloved in his own time for his artistic skills. So in that year Pope Julius II summoned Raphael to Rome to execute paintings on the walls of the new papal library, then under construction.

Here, the young painter produced his masterpiece—the *School of Athens*. An enormous work, measuring roughly 25 by 17 feet (6.5m by 5m), it shows the great ancient philosophers congregating together in a stately ancient Roman architectural setting. In a brilliant touch, the artist made several of the figures look like painters of his own day. The figure of Plato, for example, looks like Leonardo; and the Greek thinker Heraclitus closely resembles Michelangelo. (Raphael placed himself in the painting, too, on the far right side, the only one of the dozens of figures who stares outside the work directly at the observer.) Of Raphael's singular genius, one modern expert writes, "He had an extraordinary capacity . . . to respond to every movement in the art world, and to subsume [absorb] it within his own work."[42]

With Leonardo, Michelangelo, and Raphael, painting had reached a level of naturalism and grandeur that had clearly surpassed even the finest works of the ancient Greeks and Romans. Some young European artists were happy to go on emulating the Renaissance masters. But others wanted to express themselves in new ways. As had happened so often in the past, therefore, in the next few centuries styles continued to evolve in new directions, while retaining the significant advances the Renaissance had provided.

Early Modern Times: The Triumph of Emotion

I n the centuries immediately following the Renaissance, Europe remained the world's hub of major accomplishments in most arts, including painting. Painters were at work in other parts of the globe during those years, to be sure. But most of the rich art patrons, collectors, and critics were in Europe, where, thanks to the Renaissance, the institution of painting had greatly advanced.

Not surprisingly, therefore, Renaissance styles, subjects, and techniques continued to influence painters in the post-Renaissance years. In fact, art historians point out that most painting periods and styles that evolved from about 1600 to the late 1800s in one way or another echoed the visual themes and methods or at least the spirit of Renaissance painting. Nevertheless, each of these styles, which included Baroque, Rococo, Neoclassical, and Romantic, possessed attributes and visual, thematic, and technical elements that differentiated it from the others.

In general, these early modern painting periods or movements reflected artists' attempts to depict or capture human emotions, or else to appeal to the art observer's emotions. The new periods and styles were also characterized by the liberation of artists from various restrictions of the past. During the medieval

Rubens's *The Garden of Love* was indicative of the Baroque period that embraced a style meant to inspire passion and emotion through the use of rich colors. It is marked by contrasts between light and darkness with a dramatic and even chaotic look.

era, including the Renaissance, most painters, even the great Michelangelo, were not completely free to choose whatever subjects they wanted. Financial support and social acceptance for painters came mostly from the church or from royalty and nobles who largely followed the artistic whims of the Vatican. By the early 1600s, however, several Protestant churches had broken away from the Catholic Church, which as a result had lost much prestige and authority. John Graham tells how this and certain technical factors had freed painters to be as creative as they pleased.

By the 17th century, the restrictive support of the church was largely past [and] there was no limit to what artists could produce and clients were willing to be persuaded what to buy. Oils on canvases were [the rage] and the new techniques of perspective, realism, and [naturalistic] lighting were all invoked. [For painters] it was a new age of enlightenment and fun on the canvas.[43]

"A Riot of Color"

The Baroque period, lasting from the early seventeenth to early eighteenth centuries, is a good example of this "fun on the canvas." As Western painters began moving away from the structured, formal, usually well-planned and serene appearance of Renaissance art, they embraced a look meant to inspire emotion and passion. Baroque paintings most often displayed rich, deep colors, marked contrasts between light and darkness, and in many cases a dramatic, busy, even chaotic look. "This was the new style of exuberance [excitement]," one art expert points out, "where compositions were asymmetrically [unevenly] crowded with movement and action. The cool classicism of the Renaissance had been transformed into a riot of color and activity."[44]

Exactly how Baroque emotions and activity were portrayed depended in part on where in Europe the artist lived and worked. Indeed, the subjects of paintings in northern Europe during the period frequently differed from those in Italy in the south. This trend was caused largely by changing political, economic, and religious circumstances. For example, in the 1600s and 1700s the larger cities in northern Europe began to overshadow those along the Mediterranean in both trade and overseas expansion, and thereby in wealth and influence.

Also, most of the people in the northern countries had become Protestant. At first, part of the Protestant churches' reaction against Catholic traditions in Italy and elsewhere was a rejection of art having religious themes. So the bulk of northern Baroque paintings depicted themes from everyday life. These included realistic still lifes, scenes showing members of the lower classes at work and play, seascapes, cityscapes, and so forth.

From Rubens to Rembrandt

Strongly exemplifying the northern Baroque style was Peter Paul Rubens, born in what is now Belgium in 1577. His works display a wide range of rich colors. They also show characters caught in the midst of dramatic or violent situations to which they respond with fear, despair, sadness, and/or other forceful emotions.

In addition, several of Rubens's paintings illustrate the chaotic, action-filled look of many Baroque works. Excellent examples that combine all of these qualities are his *Fall of the Rebel Angels* (1622) and *The Rape of the Daughters of Leucippus* (1618). The latter shows the mythical Greco-Roman men Castor and Pollux abducting two naked young women. In a veritable mass of movement, the victims' arms and legs flail, one of the men nearly falls from his horse, and a second horse rears up, as if spooked by the commotion. Similarly, in *Rebel Angels* almost a dozen figures, including a giant serpent, writhe furiously in the midst of a desperate battle between the forces of good and evil.

Other northern European Baroque painters of note included Holland's Jan Brueghal (BREW-gul) the Elder (born 1568) and Frans Hals the Elder (circa 1580); the Belgian Jacob Jordaens (b. 1593); and Anthony van Dyck (b. 1599), who was born in what is now Belgium but worked mostly in England. Rubens, Jordaens, Van Dyck, and several other northern Baroque masters did much of their work for wealthy patrons, including princes, kings, dukes, and other nobles across the continent. So these artists became rich.

One of the greatest northern Baroque painters also made a lot of money from painting commissions but squandered much of it by living beyond his means. He was Dutchman Rembrandt van Rijn (born 1606), known to posterity by his first name. He evoked human emotions in large degree through the striking use of light, which became the chief element of his paintings. Often Rembrandt made his main subjects look more dramatic and important by placing them in a shaft or pool of light while the rest of the scene was in the shadows. A

Rembrandt's *Philosopher in Meditation* is typical of his work, in which he places subjects in a shaft or pool of light while the rest of the work is immersed in shadows or darkness.

good example is *Philosopher in Meditation* (1632), which shows an old man sitting in a room beside a window. Bright sunlight enters through the window, illuminating him and the wall behind him, while the rest of the room fades into dark shadows.

Caravaggio and Southern Baroque

The same kind of lighting effects characterized the works of Italian painter Michelangelo Merisi da Caravaggio (born 1571), one of the chief proponents of Baroque painting in southern Europe. His use of intensely contrasting light and shade became known as chiaroscuro (key-ar-oh-SKOO-roh). "By dramatically contrasting light and shade," Elke Linda Buchholz explains, "Caravaggio animated the scene producing an effect of emotional tension." In his works, she adds, "light played a dynamic role that had been, during the Renaissance, reserved for the human body."[45]

Caravaggio's choice of subjects was also noteworthy. First, he frequently chose to paint people in a manner so realistic

THE MASTER OF CHIAROSCURO

One of the finest and most influential painters of the European Renaissance, Michelangelo Merisi da Caravaggio, was born in Milan in 1571. He studied there under the respected painter Simone Peterzano, and then at the age of twenty journeyed to Rome to pursue a painting career. It did not take him long to become friendly with Francesco Maria del Monte, a powerful cardinal with a reputation for sleazy activities in his personal life. Caravaggio completed several paintings for Monte, among them *The Fortune Teller*, *The Card Players*, and *The Lute Player*. In 1606 the young painter was accused of murder after killing a man in a street brawl and fleeing first to Naples and later to the island of Malta to escape justice. While in Naples he painted his renowned *Madonna of the Rosary*. Caravaggio was best known for his dramatic visual effects, mostly created using chiaroscuro, the technique of using strongly contrasting light and dark areas in a painting. His most famous example is the powerful shaft of light in his *The Calling of St. Matthew*, produced circa 1597. He died of malaria in 1610 at the age of thirty-nine.

Caravaggio's The Calling of Saint Matthew *shows the use of contrasting light and darkness typical of chiaroscuro.*

that many observers viewed them as gritty, unflattering, or even vulgar. One irate contemporary critic charged that he was "born to destroy the art of the painting."[46] Second, because he was a Catholic working in Italy, Caravaggio did not shrink from portraying religious subjects. Biblical and spiritual themes were common in his paintings as well as in those of his colleagues and followers (called "Caravaggesques" or "Caravaggisti"). They became increasingly numerous as he grew to be one of the most influential artists of the period.

Caravaggio combined his bold use of contrasting light and shade with a strong religious subject in *The Calling of Saint Matthew* (1598), widely viewed as his masterpiece. As H.W. Janson describes it,

> Caravaggio took a bold step. He painted a story from the life of Christ as if it were happening right then and there in a Roman tavern. [Jesus] appears on the right . . . [and] as he raises his arm in a beckoning gesture, a golden beam of sunlight falls through the window behind him and carries his call across to Matthew [who is sitting at a table on the left]. This beam is by far the most important thing in the picture. Take it away, and all the magic, all the expressive power, disappears with it. . . . It is [Caravaggio's] discovery of light as *a force* that raises this tavern scene to the level of a sacred event.[47]

Other important Italian Baroque painters included Annibale Carracci (born 1560), Artemisia Gentilesqui (b. 1593), and Andrea Pozzo (b. 1642). Gentilesqui was one of the few successful female Baroque painters. Her exquisite paintings strongly resemble Caravaggio's in the use of chiaroscuro and the way both grouped their subjects. Pozzo, like so many other Baroque painters, was a master of the use of light. His *Apotheosis of St. Ignatius* (1694), applied to the ceiling of a church in Rome, is a remarkable masterwork in which he merged real architectural features with painted ones. All, along with dozens of floating human figures in brightly colored outfits, are bathed in a splendid wash of seemingly divine light.

From Rococo to Neoclassical

As had occurred so often in the past, over time both artists and the public grew tired of paintings produced in the current popular style, and the approach that replaced it provided a marked contrast. In this case, the grandiose and audacious Baroque was supplanted by the smaller-scale and far less imposing Rococo. The Rococo style, which came into fashion in the early eighteenth century, was lighter, less serious, prettier, and more playful than what had come before.

A good example of a Rococo courting scene is *The Swing* (1767) by French painter Jean-Honore Fragonard (born 1732). It depicts an apparently carefree young woman wearing an elegant dress and swinging back and forth in a quiet grove. Her smiling suitor, who lounges on the ground nearby, flirts with her while one of her slippers unexpectedly flies off her foot into the air.

Another of the more popular Rococo painters was Englishman Thomas Gainsborough (born 1727). His *Morning Walk*, painted in 1760, shows a man and woman, both well-dressed, strolling through a park along with their dog. The work was a commission to celebrate a recent marriage, so the people in the picture were not invented or fictional but rather a real couple.

Though pleasant and graceful, Rococo turned out to be one of history's shortest painting periods. During the second half of the 1700s it was largely replaced by the Neoclassical era and style. *Neo* means "new," so Neoclassical painters, like their Renaissance predecessors, tried to revive themes, ideas, and images from Greco-Roman civilization. One of their chief sources of inspiration was the excavation of the ancient Roman cities of Pompeii and Herculaneum in the mid-1700s. No one had seen these buildings or the magnificent paintings on their walls since they had been buried under tons of ash after Mt. Vesuvius erupted back in A.D. 79.

Another major inspiration for Neoclassical painters was the emergence of the European Enlightenment. That highly influential intellectual movement, which had begun in the 1600s,

Fragonard produced several paintings showing young women on swings. Whereas the most famous one, *The Swing*, completed in 1767, depicts its subjects up close, this one places them at a much more distant vantage.

swept through Europe and the Americas in the 1700s. Itself strongly shaped by ancient Greek philosophical and political concepts, the Enlightenment promoted a number of modern, progressive ideas. They included newly discovered scientific facts about Earth and the universe, religious toleration, the existence of certain basic natural human rights, and fair, democratic government. Intellectuals and others, among them the American founding fathers and the brave men and women who set the French Revolution in motion in 1789, felt lifted up and ennobled by Enlightenment ideas. So did the Neoclassical artists, including painters. They saw in the American and French Revolutions a renewal of the best aspects of ancient classical civilization and sought to glorify it in their pictures.

The foremost European Neoclassical painter was France's Jacques-Louis David (dah-VEED, born 1748). Like many of his colleagues in the genre, he often depicted scenes from Greco-Roman history and mythology. His *Intervention of the*

Sabine Women (1799), for instance, shows the famous episode from early Roman lore in which a group of women stop a battle between their Sabine fathers and brothers and new Roman husbands. Looming behind the women and soldiers, adding appropriate atmosphere, is David's impression of Rome's walls and temples. Similar carefully constructed ancient architectural renderings also appear in his renowned *Oath of the Horatii* (1785) and *Brutus Condemning His Son* (1789).

Enter the Romantics

The last of the major early modern painting periods or movements, Romanticism, spanning much of the 1800s, to a considerable degree overlapped the Neoclassical era. That is, for several years a number of painters from each movement worked and enjoyed success at the same time. In part this was because the two styles were visually very similar. Both employed painstaking realism, a fascination for historical and mythological themes, and a dramatic flair. The main difference was that the Romantics felt that Neoclassical works were too rational and objective, meaning they did not involve, explore, or commit enough to human emotions. So in a sense, Romanticism was a sort of triumph of emotion over reason. Enrico Annosica explains:

> Romanticism had less clearly defined outlines [than Neoclassicism]. It was an indication of mood as well as taste, a collective expression of the prevailing European spirit—often accompanied by a degree of extreme emotion. . . . The Romantics went further than the Neoclassical artists would ever have contemplated, even though both were searching for the same truths about the human soul. [The Romantics] attempted to explore a deeper, darker level of the human spirit. . . . The occult [supernatural], the significance of dreams, notions of infinity [eternal things], a yearning for distant, exotic lands, anxiety, and the predominance of emotions were among the wide variety of themes that concerned the Romantics.[48]

One of the chief ways that the Romantics explored these darker or more exotic themes was through very atmospheric depictions of natural settings. Usually, but certainly not always, one or more people stood or struggled within these tortured landscapes. An excellent example is *Wanderer Above a Sea of Fog* (circa 1818) by German painter Caspar David Friedrich (born 1774). A man, possibly intended to represent the artist himself, stands alone atop a craggy peak, staring out at massive billows of deep mist enshrouding the valley below. His back turned to the observer, who is left to wonder what the lonesome figure is thinking, he seems to symbolize a larger humanity attempting to regain a lost connection with nature. In fact, as scholar Irina Stotland points out, Friedrich and other Romantics "believed that nature's spiritual power could help man[kind] to better understand life."[49]

The Romantic style explored more exotic scenes through atmospheric depictions of landscapes with one or more figures standing within. Casper David Friedrich's *Wanderer Above a Sea of Fog* is a fine example of this style.

Other leading Romantic artists included France's Theodore Géricault (jair-i-KOH, born 1774) and Eugène Delacroix (d'la-KWA, b. 1798); England's J.M.W. Turner (b. 1775) and John Constable (b. 1776); and Spain's Francisco Goya (b. 1746). Some of them explored not only mystical nature and human spiritual elements, but also political themes that captured strong or even violent feelings. Géricault's 1819 work, *The Raft of the Medusa*, set the standard for this sub-genre of Romanticism. It portrays a real event in which several people were abandoned on a raft at sea after a shipwreck, an incident covered up by the French government. The height of Romantic political painting came later with Delacroix's masterpiece,

THE REAL RAFT OF THE MEDUSA

French Romantic painter Theodore Géricault's The Raft of the Medusa, *created in 1819, depicts a group of people suffering and dying on a raft drifting in the ocean. It was in large degree a critical statement against the French government for its cover-up of a shameful incident involving officers of the country's navy three years before. Noted art historian Robert Cumming provides this brief overview of the circumstances of the incident, which eventually became a public scandal.*

I n the summer of 1816, a French frigate, the *Medusa*, was wrecked off the coast of Africa while carrying soldiers and settlers to the Colony of Senegal. The incompetent captain was a nobleman who gained his position through political influence. When the ship was wrecked, he was on one of the few lifeboats, leaving the people he saw as his social inferiors to fend for themselves. Those 149 men (and one woman) built a makeshift raft and were adrift for thirteen days. Only 15 survived the horrendous circumstances, and instances of cannibalism and insanity were reported. Five more died on reaching land.

Robert Cumming. *Annotated Art*. New York: Dorling Kindersley, 1995, p. 77.

Theodore Géricault's The Raft of the Medusa *was based on actual events.*

Liberty Leading the People (1830). Celebrating the great Paris uprising of 1830, it shows a bare-breasted woman, representing liberty, leading armed revolutionaries over the bodies of fallen patriots.

The Romantic movement brought Western painting to the height of realistic imagery and emotional expression. It was unclear to some art critics, as well as many of the artists themselves, where the art of painting might or even could go from there. The answer to this quandary did not take long to materialize. The last decades of the nineteenth century witnessed the emergence of styles that reacted against, and at times cast aside, strict realism. The birth of so-called modern art was at hand.

The Modern Era: An Explosion of Bold New Styles

For many centuries leading up to the Renaissance and during the initial centuries following it, painters had striven for increased visual realism. But beginning in the second half of the nineteenth century this fairly abruptly changed. No longer were the leading painters concerned with reproducing as best as they could the natural look of people, animals, and objects. Instead, they either captured the mere essences of those subjects or used paint in an abstract, ill-defined way to express their own beliefs or inner feelings. As a result, most so-called modern art tends not to resemble art from earlier ages.

Exactly why and how this far-reaching change in painting occurred is still not completely understood. A number of factors appear to have caused it, one consisting of an effort by artists of all types to seek new, fresher ways of describing the natural world. In a way, it was an attempt to look below reality's surface to find its inner, mostly invisible qualities. In Hans L.C. Jaffe's words, painters

> sought the new reality on a plane that lies behind, beneath, and beyond appearances—a plane on which the appearance of things is more likely to be concealed than revealed. What had to be done was to pierce the veil of visible appearance—not passive reporting of the

eye's experience, but instead, through intellectual and spiritual effort, the construction of a new conception of reality.[50]

Art historians say that another factor that helped to shape the look of modern art was the invention of photography in the 1800s. Before this major technological advance, one expert explains, a person

> who wished to perpetuate something, to preserve at least a record of its outer semblance, had no one to turn to save the painter. . . . But then, with the coming of the camera, anyone who wished to preserve such a likeness could turn to the photographer as well. [This brought about] a change in the limits of what had been the painter's special domain.[51]

Many painters viewed photography as a competitor in the business of reproducing images of the natural world. More-over, they increasingly felt the camera was a rival they could not effectively compete with. So they began to move away from portraying the world in strictly realistic ways and to ex-periment with more intangible, or abstract, images. Whatever their reasons may have been, many modern painters veered off in numerous different directions, creating bold new styles. "From the death of naturalism," Roy Bolton remarks, "came an explosion of movements, often pulling in [opposite] directions, which explored the new possibilities that an art without limits could throw up."[52]

The Impressionists

The first major new modern painting style quickly came to be called Impressionism. This was because the term was so apt and descriptive. As John Graham says, "The word stands for itself. Rather than painting detailed pictures, Impressionists wanted only to paint an impression of what they saw, whose details the viewer would complete. Thus, each viewer might see something slightly different."[53] Florens Deuchler agrees, writing, "The Impressionists do not seek to reproduce the actual structure of objects, but to show them at a given moment under certain conditions of light and atmosphere."[54]

In their attempts to capture only the essence of people and objects, the Impressionists developed an overall look frequently described as sketchy, rough, or even unfinished. Yet it was also filled with eye-catching color. In addition, Impressionists played with depicting the way light falls on and reveals objects in ways that most earlier artists rarely attempted. They explored "the effects of light and color on the mind," an art historian points out.

> In bright sunshine, color, depth, and detail can be blurred out, leaving only flashes of color. The Impressionists painted these flashes, thickly pasted onto the canvas in a way that left little room for unnecessary details. By the way they painted, with palette-knives, fingers, or anything that could push the paint around in the way they wanted, they also created a second aesthetic [artistic quality] to their paintings—the texture and feeling of the paint itself became a subject of beauty.[55]

This sketchy, blurred, and/or textured look is well-illustrated in the works of one of the leading early Impressionists, Frenchman Claude Monet (moh-NAY, born 1840). In 1890 he purchased a house in Giverny, in northern France, a property covered with lovely gardens and a lily pond. These natural wonders inspired him and became some of his principal subjects. Often he painted the same area or scene repeatedly in different seasons or times of the day to capture changing lighting effects and moods.

Monet's most famous paintings are his studies of water lilies, which evolved in appearance and technique over the years. His 1906 *Water Lilies*, for instance, shows a predominantly sky blue pond surface dotted with light blue and blue-green splotches representing the lilies. The brush strokes are fairly subtle and the edges of the lilies largely blur and blend with the water. In contrast, his 1920 *Water Lilies* is considerably

Impressionist painter Claude Monet's most famous paintings depict water lilies. He produced forty-eight paintings of water lilies that reveal the evolution of his techniques. This painting was completed in 1906.

sketchier, with bolder, rougher brushstrokes. The later painting is also alive with a broader range of colors, including pink, red, and yellow ochre. In all, Monet produced forty-eight paintings of water lilies, each viewed today as a masterpiece. He also painted twenty pictures of the facade of Rouen Cathedral at different times of the day, each exploring subtle differences in lighting.

Other leading Impressionists included France's Camille Pissarro (born 1830), Edgar Degas (b. 1834), Pierre-Auguste Renoir (b. 1841), and George Seurat (b. 1859); Vincent van Gogh (van-GOH in American English, b. 1853) of the Netherlands; Norway's Edvard Munch (b. 1863); and James Whistler (b. 1834) of the United States. Of these, the oldest, Pissarro, was also the most widely influential on other Impressionists in their era. His lush depictions of Paris street scenes feature hundreds of thick dabs of color that together portray highly atmospheric lighting schemes.

Another in this group of masters, Van Gogh, employed a similar but more exaggerated technique, with bolder, broader brushstrokes and a larger array of bright colors. Also, his skies and backgrounds are often alive with abstract swirls of light and color, producing a surreal, or dreamlike, effect. The most famous example is his *Starry Night* (1889), depicting a village in the distance in the evening. The sky looming behind the village is filled with blurry swirls representing the moon and stars. This technique and look daringly challenges the viewer with a vision of what the artist might have seen as an alternate reality beneath the surface of normality. Whatever one thinks of Van Gogh's distinctive style, today his works are worth a fortune. His painting *Dr. Gachet* (1890) sold at auction in 1990 for the incredible sum of $83 million.

Van Gogh's technique was more exaggerated, using bolder, and broader brushstrokes and bright colors that produced a surreal effect. His masterpiece *Starry Night* shows an alternate reality beneath a surface of normality.

Enter the Cubists

Impressionism proved to be only the opening salvo in a true revolution in the art of painting that gained steam in the early decades of the twentieth century. Most of the art styles or movements of the 1900s abandoned literal depictions of people and objects in the natural world. Rather, many leading painters explored the underlying meanings of the universe or existence or used their art to make personal statements about their feelings and emotions. One noted painter summarized this approach, saying, "The method of painting is the natural growth out of a need. I want to express my feelings rather than illustrate them. Technique is just a means of arriving at a statement."[56]

Another important aspect of the movements and styles following Impressionism is that they have been very numerous and have quite often overlapped one another. Creating even more confusion for average observers, art historians have at times differed on what marks one modern style as different from the others. But the fact is that such differences are mainly academic and understood only by a handful of art specialists and collectors. Average people with little or no knowledge of art usually cannot tell one modern style from another. As a result, the majority of modern paintings are often lumped together under convenient but nonspecific labels like "avant-garde" (meaning "at the forefront") or "abstract."

The first and foremost of these modern styles, which in many ways influenced and broke ground for most of the later ones, came to be called Cubism. It was at first primarily the brainchild of Spain's Pablo Picasso (born 1881), whom many experts have called the most important artist of the twentieth century. (In addition to his enormous talent as a painter, he was a gifted sculptor, potter, and printmaker.)

In 1906 Picasso's friend, French painter Henri Matisse (1869), who began as an Impressionist, showed him a small piece of sculpture made in Africa. Seeing the work as pleasantly strange and disjointed in its depiction of the human form, Picasso was swept away with inspiration for a new approach to

The Scream, *by Norwegian artist Edvard Munch, became one of the most famous and in certain ways disquieting early modern paintings. It shows a gaunt person with a skeletal head standing on a bridge and covering his ears with his hands. His eyes and mouth are wide open, and it seems clear that he is indeed screaming in utter torment. Moreover, his anguish appears to be reflected in the starkly weird landscape looming behind him with its lurid red and yellow sky. But why, many observers have queried over the years, is the figure in the picture so distressed? What was Munch trying to get across with this plainly disturbing image? To this day most people who see photos of the painting are unaware that the artist explained it rather clearly in a note in his diary. It reads,*

I was walking along a path with two friends. The sun was setting [and] suddenly the sky turned blood red. I paused, feeling exhausted, and leaned on the fence. There was blood and tongues of fire above the blue-

black fjord [inlet of the sea] and the city. My friends walked on, and I stood there trembling with anxiety, and I sensed an infinite scream passing through nature.

Quoted in Moodbook.com. "Edvard Munch." www.moodbook.com/history/modernism/edvard-munch-scream.html.

Norwegian artist Edvard Munch's The Scream *was inspired by a personal experience during a sunset.*

European sculpture and painting. He immediately got to work with his paints and created several experimental canvases.

The final version of this series of paintings is the now classic *Les Demoiselles d'Avignon* (*The Young Ladies of Avignon*), 1907. It depicts five naked women with their bodies divided into distinct wedge-shaped sections. Some observers have quipped that it looks like someone had sliced up the women and done a poor job of putting the pieces back together. Yet the overall image was and remains powerful and compelling. As Wendy Beckett describes it and Cubism in general,

> It is almost impossible to overestimate the importance of this picture and the profound effect it had on art subsequently. The savage, inhuman heads of the figures are the direct result of Picasso's recent exposure to tribal art, but it is what he does with their heads—the wild, almost reckless freedom with which he incorporates them into his own personal vision . . . that gives the picture its awesome force. . . . [He] chose to break down the subjects . . . into a number of facets, showing several different aspects of one [woman] simultaneously.[57]

Pablo Picasso's 1907 painting *Les Demoiselles d'Avignon*, with its disjointed women, was the founding example of Cubism.

THE BRILLIANT AND RESTLESS PICASSO

Often called the most original, important, and influential artist of the twentieth century, Pablo Picasso was born in Malaga, Spain, in 1881. His father, who was a painter, taught him to draw and quickly found that the boy was extraordinarily talented. In fact, the elder Picasso was said to have remarked that Pablo had completely surpassed him in painting ability at the tender age of thirteen. As an adult artist in his own right, Picasso spent most of this time working in France. By all accounts he was a brilliant, endlessly energetic, restless individual who constantly searched for new ways to express himself artistically. For that reason, he delved not only into painting but also into sculpture, ceramics, printmaking, and several other creative genres. He also had a hand in nearly every artistic movement in the century. Art historians have broken down his work into periods, including his Blue period (1901–1904), Rose period (1905–1907), and Negro period (1907–1909). In the latter he produced paintings that initiated the Cubist movement. Picasso's personal life was marked by numerous intense relationships with women, some of whom he married and others who became his mistresses. They all became subjects of his artworks, which numbered in the thousands. Both before and after his death (in 1973), his paintings garnered enormous prices. The largest was for his 1932 work *Nude, Green Leaves and Bust*, which sold at auction in 2010 for a whopping $106.5 million.

The "Noise" of Life

Part of the "profound effect" of Cubism on later art that Beckett mentions was the emergence of so-called Futurism, which was popular from roughly 1910 to the early 1940s. (Early Futurists are still sometimes called "Cubo-Futurists" because of their connection to Cubism.) The painters and other artists in that movement identified themselves with the future—meaning the modern age and where it might lead—because they strongly rejected past artistic ideas and traditions. A leading early Futurist, Italy's Umberto Boccioni (born 1882), stated fervently,

> We rebel against that spineless worshipping of old canvases, old statues and old bric-a-brac, against everything which is filthy and worm-ridden and corroded by time. We consider the habitual contempt for everything which is young, new and burning with life to be unjust and even criminal.[58]

Boccioni and other Futurists tried to depict the fast-paced, energetic, even violent aspects of modern life in their paintings. In particular, they were fascinated by technology, including fast machines such as cars, motorcycles, and airplanes. They also attempted, to the extent it was possible, to visually portray the sounds of machines, as well as of life in general. A good example is Boccioni's *The Laugh* (1911), in which a mass of jumbled images creates the feeling of dynamic movement and in a sense the "noise" of life. A female Cubo-Futurist, Russian artist Liubov Popova (born 1889), achieved a similar effect in her work *The Philosopher* (1915), a stunning juxtaposition of partial images and shapes.

Among the many other short-lived but important twentieth-century painting styles and movements, one of the most famous was called Surrealism. Like the Futurists had, its members reacted against the existing world. But the Surrealists wanted in a sense to look below the world's and society's surfaces and try to discover unseen qualities they felt were usually revealed only in dreams or other manifestations of the subconscious mind. This, they hoped, would give them insights into the surreal, or "more real," aspects of life. The movement thrived in Europe from the 1920s through the 1940s and spread to other parts of the world, including Japan.

Probably the most famous Surrealist was Spaniard Salvador Dalí (born 1904). His paintings, which over the decades

Liubov Popov's *The Philosopher* shows the juxtaposition of partial images and shapes common in Cubo-Futurist paintings.

have been used in book covers, posters, and movies, to name only a few other mediums, colorfully took everyday objects and distorted them in various ways. An often-cited example is *The Persistence of Memory* (1931), which shows watches melting. Evidently it was Dalí's attempt to suggest that time is meaningless in the surreal world beneath life's surface.

Another Surrealist, Mexico's Frida Kahlo (born 1907), explored the unseen world beneath her own skin. After suffering serious injuries in a car accident when she was a teenager, she became obsessed with expressing the depth of her agonies through her art. In a kind of morbid self-portrait, *The Broken Column* (1944) shows her facing the viewer, with her broken spine visible in a cut-away in the center of her body. Similarly, *The Two Fridas* (1939) displays two images of her, each with the heart, arteries and all, floating outside her body atop her dress. Despite the obviously dreamlike setting of the work, Kahlo herself insisted, "I have never painted dreams. I painted my reality."[59]

Contemporary Art and the Future

The Impressionists, Cubists, Futurists, and Surrealists at least attempted, in their individual ways, to portray real people and objects. Quite a few modern artists did not even try. Their works, which fell into various abstract styles, including so-called Abstract Expressionism, used paint in much vaguer and less defined ways. One of the most renowned abstract painters was an American, Jackson Pollock (born 1912). He gained international fame for his "drip" paintings, made by spreading his canvas on the floor and dripping, sprinkling, or flinging his paint onto its surface. Among his numerous works, which today fetch enormous prices in the art collectors' world, are *Number 7A* (1948) and *Number 22* (1950).

Many painters still copy Pollock's style, while numerous others continue to imitate the Pop art genre pioneered by Americans Andy Warhol (born 1928) and Jasper Johns (b. 1930). In general, Pop artists take objects or images from the real world and either use them in an artistic setting or literally turn them into art. Warhol, for instance, gained widespread fame for utilizing the commercial image of a Campbell's soup can in his works. Johns did something similar with the image of the American flag.

Johns is still alive and producing art. (In 2006 two collectors bought his *False Start* for $80 million, the largest amount ever paid to a living painter for a single work.) That makes him a Contemporary artist, at least by one definition of the term *Contemporary art*, namely, art that is presently being created. A more general definition for the term, preferred by most museums, is all modern art created since World War II (1939-1945).

Contemporary artist Jasper Johns is well known for his Pop art creations that incorporate the American flag.

Within that broad grouping of artists and their works are painters who work in almost all the styles of the present and past. Some prefer to turn out realistic images like those of the Renaissance, Baroque, and Neoclassical periods. Others carry on the Impressionist tradition with its endless plays of light and color. Still others choose to reject past styles and experiment with new ones. In the meantime, the advent of a wide range of electronic media has tended to cause art of several styles and periods to be incorporated together in new forms of artistic expression. "Since the 1960s," art historian Karoline Hille points out, "the expansion of artistic possibilities . . . via photography and videography has changed [art] at [its] very foundations and has promoted the integration [combination] of all forms of art."[60]

Only one thing can be said for certain about the future of painting, and that is that no longer will a new style arrive and remain the norm for one, two, or more centuries. As the twentieth century demonstrated, technology has made the world move faster. Art styles came and went rapidly in that century, and experts think that trend will continue, at least for the near future. In Hille's words, "Contemporary art reflects the fast-paced world [we live in]. Styles and movements are born and disappear at the speed of the information age."[61]

Notes

Introduction: A Mirror of Human Culture

1. Robert Cumming. *Annotated Art.* New York: Dorling Kindersley, 1995, p. 9.
2. John Graham. *A Short History of Painting.* Scotts Valley, CA: CreateSpace, 2008, p. 36
3. Graham. *A Short History of Painting*, p. 39.
4. Hans L.C. Jaffe. *The History of World Painting.* London: New Orchard Editions, 1985, p. 13.

Chapter 1: The Earliest Civilizations: The Dawn of Painting

5. Quoted in International Committee for Preservation of Lascaux. "Finding Lascaux: Four Boys and a Dog." www.savelascaux.org/Legacy_Finding.php.
6. Quoted in International Committee for Preservation of Lascaux. "Finding Lascaux."
7. Andrew Howley. "70th Anniversary of the Discovery of Lascaux." National Geographic. http://news watch.nationalgeographic.com/201 0/09/17/70th_anniversary_lascaux.

8. Roy Bolton. *A Brief History of Painting.* London: Magpie, 2004, p. 1.
9. Dianne Durante. "Egyptian Painting." Beyond Books.com. www.be yond books.com/art11/2b.asp.
10. Enrico Annosica et al. *Art: A World History.* London: Dorling Kindersley, 1999, pp. 22, 24
11. Durante. "Egyptian Painting."
12. Thomas Sakoulas. "Minoan Art." Ancient-Greece.org. www.ancient-greece.org/art/minoan-art.html.
13. William R. Biers. *The Archaeology of Greece.* Ithaca, NY: Cornell University Press, 1996, pp. 44–45.
14. Wendy Beckett. *The Story of Painting.* New York: Dorling Kindersley, 2000, p. 18.
15. Sakoulas. "Minoan Art."

Chapter 2: Greece and Rome: Inventing Styles for the Ages

16. Quoted in Thucydides. *The Peloponnesian War.* Translated by Rex Warner. New York: Penguin, 2008, p. 148.
17. Bolton. *A Brief History of Painting*, p. 2.
18. Robert B. Kebric. *Greek People.* Mountain View, CA: Mayfield, 2001, p. 140.
19. Vitruvius. *On Architecture.* Vol. 2. Translated by Frank Granger. Cambridge,

MA: Harvard University Press, 2002, p. 71.

20. Lucian. *Zeuxis and Antiochus*. Translated by H.W. Fowler. Internet Sacred Text Archive. www.sacred-texts .com/cla/luc/wl2/wl207 .htm.

21. Pliny the Elder. *Pliny the Elder: Natural History: A Selection*. Translated by John H. Healy. New York: Penguin, 1991, p. 333.

22. Richard and Deborah Zuccarini. "Fresco History and Technique." *Sacred Art Journal*, vol. 13, 1992, pp. 104–105.

23. Josephus. *The Jewish War*. Translated by G.A. Williamson. New York: Penguin, 2000, p. 385.

Chapter 3: Beyond the West: Masterworks Across the Globe

24. Annosica. *Art: A World History*, pp. 168–169.

25. Bolton. *A Brief History of Painting*, p. 3.

26. Jaffe. *The History of World Painting*, p. 366.

27. Quoted in Culturekiosque. "Ancient Maya Mural at San Bartolo, Guatemala Tells Story of Myths and Kings." www.culturekiosque .com/art/news/maya_mural_san_ bartolo_guatemala.html.

Chapter 4: Europe's Renaissance: The Zenith of Realism

28. Elke Linda Buchholz. "Renaissance." In Elke Linda Buchholz et al. *Art: A World History*. New York: Abrams, 2007, p. 122.

29. Bolton. *A Brief History of Painting*, p. 19.

30. H.W. Janson and Dora Jane Janson. *The Story of Painting: From Cave Painting to Modern Times*. New York: Abrams, 1999, p. 28.

31. Susanne Kaepelle. "Late Antiquity and the Middle Ages." In Buchholz et al. *Art: A World History*, p. 94.

32. Jaffe. *The History of World Painting*, p. 106.

33. Beckett. *The Story of Painting*, p. 61.

34. Beckett. *The Story of Painting*, p. 61.

35. Bolton. *A Brief History of Painting*, p. 24.

36. Bolton. *A Brief History of Painting*, p. 24.

37. Buchholz. "Renaissance," p. 120.

38. Charles L. Mee Jr. *Daily Life in Renaissance Italy*. New York: American Heritage, 1975, p. 92.

39. Quoted in Florens Deuchler. *A Short History of Painting: From Cave Art to Jackson Pollock*. New York: Abrams, 1968, p. 43.

40. Deuchler. *A Short History of Painting*, p. 47.

41. Cumming. *Annotated Art*, p. 31.

42. Beckett. *The Story of Painting*, p. 218.

Chapter 5: Early Modern Times: The Triumph of Emotion

43. Graham. *A Short History of Painting*, p. 20.

44. Bolton. *A Brief History of Painting*, p. 96.

45. Elke Linda Buchholz. "Baroque." In Buchholz et al. *Art: A World History*, pp. 218, 220.

46. Quoted in Buchholz. "Baroque," p. 220.

47. Janson. *The Story of Painting*, pp. 86, 88–89.

48. Annosica. *Art*, pp. 372–373.

49. Irina Stotland. "Nineteenth Century." In Buchholz et al. *Art: A World History*, p. 326.

Chapter 6: The Modern Era: An Explosion of Bold New Styles

50. Jaffe. *The History of World Painting*, p. 290.

51. Jaffe. *The History of World Painting*, p. 289.

52. Bolton. *A Brief History of Painting*, p. 220.

53. Graham. *A Short History of Painting*, p. 21.

54. Deuchler. *A Short History of Painting*, p. 126.

55. Bolton. *A Brief History of Painting*, p. 196.

56. Quoted in The Warhol. "Artists Past and Present: Jackson Pollock." http://edu.warhol.org/app_pollock. html.

57. Beckett. *The Story of Painting*, pp. 641, 644.

58. Quoted in Artinthepicture.com. "What Is Futurism?" www.artinthepicture.com/styles/Futurism.

59. Quoted in Buchholz et al. *Art: A World History*, p. 452.

60. Karoline Hille. "Art After 1945." In Buchholz et al. *Art: A World History*, p. 470.

61. Hille. "Art After 1945," p. 500.

Glossary

aesthetic: Relating to emotions, feelings, and/or artistic impulses.

antiquity: Ancient times.

chiaroscuro: In painting, the use of intensely contrasting effects of light and shade.

cinnabar: Mercury sulfide; a mineral traditionally used to make red pigment for paints.

classical: Greco-Roman.

Contemporary art: Art that is presently being produced; or according to some authorities all art created since 1945.

conventions: Traditional, accepted rules and techniques.

emakimono (or *emaki*): In traditional Japan, rolls of paper on which artists painted images to illustrate text; or the technique of painting on such rolls.

fresco: A painting done on wet plaster.

illuminated manuscript (or illumination): In medieval Europe, an illustrated Bible or other book.

India ink: A substance used extensively in ancient Chinese art, made by mixing carbon black with animal glues.

monumental: Large-scale.

mural: A painting, usually large, done on a wall or other permanent surface.

naturalistic: Reproducing the natural world; realistic.

palette: A thin, flat board on which a painter mixes his or her paints.

panel painting: A painting done on a piece of wood; or the art of painting on wood.

perspective: In painting, a visual impression of depth achieved by using sight lines that converge at a distant vanishing point.

secco: The technique of painting on dry plaster.

sfumato: A technique in which a painter slightly blurs the edges of objects in a picture, which adds a naturalistic look.

still life: A painting of a group of commonplace inanimate objects.

tempera: Paint made by mixing powdered pigments with glue and liquids like water or raw egg yolk.

triumphal paintings: In ancient Rome, paintings depicting battles and other war-related subjects.

Yamato-e: In traditional Japan, a national painting style that emerged in the 800s and 900s A.D.

For More Information

Books

Enrico Annosica et al. *Art: A World History*. London: Dorling Kindersley, 1999. One of the better general overviews of art history available, this volume contains numerous reproductions of important examples of painting, sculpture, architecture, and other art forms through the ages.

James Barter. *In the Glory of God: Medieval Art*. Detroit, MI: Lucent, 2006. This excellent volume aimed at junior high and high school students contains well-researched overviews of the major medieval art forms.

Wendy Beckett. *The Story of Painting*. New York: Dorling Kindersley, 2000. This beautifully illustrated volume vividly discusses all aspects of Western art in easy-to-understand wording.

Janetta R. Benton. *The Art of the Middle Ages*. London: Thames and Hudson, 2002. Benton delivers a well-rounded study of medieval art, with special emphasis placed on regional styles and achievements.

Roy Bolton. *A Brief History of Painting*. London: Magpie, 2004. In clear, concise prose, and supported by numerous beautiful reproductions of paintings, noted British art historian Bolton tells how painting developed over the centuries.

Elke Linda Buchholz et al. *Art: A World History*. New York: Abrams, 2007. Written in an easy-to-read style, this handsomely mounted book features two or more photos of major artworks on every page.

Glyn Davies and Kirstin Kennedy. *Medieval and Renaissance Art: People and Possessions*. London: V and A, 2009. Although the authors are museum curators, they do not talk down to the reader in this easy-to-understand introduction to all areas of artistic production in the Middle Ages and Renaissance.

David Franklin, ed. *Leonardo da Vinci, Michelangelo, and the Renaissance in Florence*. New Haven, CT: Yale University Press, 2005. The editor has compiled a collection of useful expert observations of the works of these two great artistic masters.

John Graham. *A Short History of Painting*. Scotts Valley, CA: CreateSpace,

2008. A brief but valuable introduction to major painting terminology, styles, and major painters.

Reynold Higgins. *Minoan and Mycenaean Art*. London: Thames and Hudson, 1997. Well researched and authoritative, this is one of the two best sources available on the subject.

H.W. Janson and Anthony F. Janson. *History of Art*. New York: Abrams, 1997. This major study of art history contains large amounts of information about the evolution of the various art forms and features numerous beautiful illustrations of examples of each form.

H.W. Janson and Dora Jane Janson. *The Story of Painting: From Cave Painting to Modern Times*. New York: Abrams, 1999. Nicely illustrated, this overview of painting history is written in a simple style that everyone, from children to adults, can readily understand.

J.J. Pollitt. *The Ancient View of Greek Art*. New Haven, CT: Yale University Press, 2009. An exceptionally good study of Greek art as seen through the eyes of the Greeks themselves.

Nancy H. Ramage. *Roman Art*. New York: Prentice Hall, 2008. This readable volume is viewed by many scholars as the best general recent study of a wide range of Roman arts.

Gay Robins, *The Art of Ancient Egypt*. Cambridge, MA: Harvard University Press, 2008. One of the leading experts on ancient Egyptian art delivers an informative, readable book.

Marilyn Stokstad. *Art: A Brief History*. Upper Saddle River, NJ: Pearson, 2009. One reviewer summed up this volume well, saying it is "easy to understand" and that it "makes it easy to learn about each period in art history." The combination of straightforward, authoritative writing and superior presentation makes this one of the best available books on art history.

Abigail Wheatley. *The Story of Painting*. London: Usborne, 2007. Aimed at young readers, this colorfully illustrated book provides a valuable introduction to the history of painting for beginners.

Websites

Artemisia Gentileschi (www.artrenewal .org/pages/artist.php?artistid=4249). A beautiful website that displays copies of most of this famous female painter's finest works.

Chinese Art (www.essentialhumanities .net/artw7.php). A useful general overview of the subject.

Cubism (www.artlex.com/ArtLex/c/cu bism.html). This online source offers brief but well-researched synopses of major art periods and forms. Click on any of the many links provided to learn about specific techniques and view famous paintings in the genre.

Egyptian Art (www.essentialhumanities .net/artw2.php). This easy-to-read introduction to Egyptian art contains numerous photos of ancient paintings, sculptures, and architectural forms.

Greek Painting (www.essentialhumani ties.net/paint2_2.php). Contains many beautiful photos of Greek paintings on vases and other surfaces.

Learn About Baroque Art (www.art history-famousartists-paintings.com/ BaroqueArt.html). This site provides a simple overview of Baroque painting, along with reproductions of famous Baroque paintings.

Michelangelo Buonarroti (www.michel angelo.com/buonarroti.html). The home page of an excellent series of web sites devoted to the life and works of one of the greatest artists who ever lived. Contains many stunning photos of his paintings, sculptures, and architectural achievements.

Romanticism (www.lilithgallery.com/ arthistory/romanticism/arthistory_ romanticism.html). An attractive, information-filled site that describes this major painting movement and provides links to several specific painters and paintings.

Index

Realism
  in Chinese art, 46
  Leonardo's contribution to, 67
  modern era and rejection of, 85
  in Neoclassical/Romantic art, 81
  in Renaissance art, 64–65
  in Roman art, 39
Reformation, 12
Rembrandt van Rijn, 74–75
Renaissance, 56, 61, 63
  influence on post-Renaissance art, 71
  trend toward realism during, 64–65
Renoir, Pierre-Auguste, 88
Rock paintings (India), *44*
Rococo style, 78–79
Romanesque period, 58–59
Romanticism, 80–84
Rome, 43
  fall of, 42, 63
  Greek tradition continued by, 38–40
  potter-painters of, 11–12
  subject of paintings in, 40
Rubens, Peter Paul, 74

S
Saint-Savin sur Gartempe (France), 59, *59*
Sakoulas, Thomas, 27
San Bartolo (Guatemala), Maya murals at, 52–53, 55
Saturno, William, 52–53
School of Athens (Raphael), 70
The Scream (Munch), 91, *91*
Secco technique, 27, 34
Seurat, George, 88
Sfumato technique, 67
Shen Chou, 48
Silvester, Hans, 51
Sistine Chapel (Rome), 68, 70
Sistine Madonna (Raphael), 69, *69*
Song dynasty, 46, 49
Starry Night (Van Gogh), 89, *89*
Stotland, Irina, 81
Surrealism, 94

The Swing (Fragonard), *79*

T
Tales of Genji, 50
T'ang Yin, *48*
Timon (Greek painter), 36, 37
Turner, J.M.W., 82
The Two Fridas (Kahlo), 96

U
Uccello, Paolo, 64, 65

V
Van Dyck, Anthony, 74
Van Eyck, Jan, 65, 66
Van Gogh, Vincent, 88, 89
Vasari, Giorgio, 64
Vases, painted, *33*
Vitruvius (Roman architect), 34–35

W
Wall paintings, *11*
  ancient, 10–12
  of Crete, *11*, 24, *24*
  See also Frescoes
Wanderer Above a Sea of Fog (Friedrich), 81, *82*
Wang Wei, 46
Warhol, Andy, 96
Water Lilies (Monet), 87–88, *88*
Wen Cheng-Ming, 48
Whistler, James, 88
Women painters, Greek, 36, 37, 38

X
Xia Gui, 49

Y
Yamato-e, 49

Z
Zeuxis (Greek painter), 32, 35–36
Zuccarini, Richard, 39–40

Picture Credits

Cover: © Odua Images/Shutterstock.com
The Art Archive, 21
The Art Archive/Bibliothèque Musèe du Louvre/Gianni Dagli Orti, 23
The Art Archive/Freer Gallery of Art, 48
The Art Archive/Gianni Dagli Orti, 38
The Art Archive/Heraklion Museum/Gianni Dagli Orti, 11, 26
The Art Archive/Museo del Prado Madrid/Collection Dagli Orti, 72
The Art Archive/National Archaeological Museum Athens/Gianni Dagli Orti, 29
The Art Archive/National Anthropological Museum Mexico/Gianni Dagli Orti, 54
The Art Archive/National Gallery of Art, Washington, 79
The Art Archive, National Palace Museum Taiwan, 47
The Art Archive/Sta Maria del Carmine, Florence Collection Dagli Orti, 60
Attic red-figure hydria, decorated with a scene of the Thracian bard Thamyris being deprived of sight and voice, from the Group of Polygnotus, c.440-420 BC, 33
Blue Monkey Fresco/Ashmolean Museum, University of Oxford, UK/The Bridgeman Art Library, 24
bpk, Berlin/Art Resource, NY, 66
© DeA Picture Library /Art Resource, NY, 19, 42
Erich Lessing/Art Resource, NY, 37, 62, 69, 75, 80, 88, 95
Flag Above White With Collage © Jasper Johns/Licensed by VAGA, New York, NY, 97
HIP/Art Resource, NY, 9
Picasso, Pablo, "Les Demoiselles D'Avignon." 1907, painting. Museum of Modern Art/The Art Archive/The Picture Desk, Inc. © 2007 Estate of Pablo Picasso/ Artists Rights Society (ARS), New York, 92
The Raft of the Medusa, 1819 (oil on canvas), Gericault, Theodore (1791-1824)/Louvre, Paris, France/The Bridgeman Art Library International, 83
Réunion des Musées Nationaux/Art Resource, NY, 67
Rock painting of a bull and horses, c.17000 BC (cave painting), Prehistoric/Caves of Lascaux, Dordogne, France/The Bridgeman Art Library International, 16
Scala/Art Resource, NY, 30
The Scream, 1893 (oil, tempera & pastel on cardboard), Munch, Edvard (1863-1944)/ Nasjonalgalleriet, Oslo, Norway/© DACS/The Bridgeman Art Library International, 91
SEF/Art Resource, NY, 53
© SuperStock/SuperStock, 82, 89
Universal Images Group/Art Resource, NY, 57
© Universal Images Group/SuperStock, 76
Vanni/Art Resource, NY, 41, 44
View of the Crypt and the Legend of St. Savin and St. Cyprien (photo), French School, (12th century)/Abbey Church, Saint-Savin-sur-Gartempe, France/Giraudon/The Bridgeman Art Library International, 59
Werner Forman/Art Resource, NY, 50

About the Author

Historian Don Nardo is best known for his books for young people about the ancient and medieval worlds. These include volumes on the arts of ancient cultures, including Mesopotamian arts and literature, Egyptian sculpture and monuments, Greek temples, Roman amphitheaters, medieval castles, and general histories of sculpture, painting, and architecture through the ages. Nardo lives with his wife, Christine, in Massachusetts.